moshi monsters™

MOSHIPEDIA
A-Z of MOSHI!

PUFFIN

PUFFIN BOOKS

Published by the Penguin Group
Penguin Books Ltd, 80 Strand, London WC2R 0RL, England
Penguin Group (USA) Inc., 375 Hudson Street, New York, New York 10014, USA
Penguin Group (Canada), 90 Eglinton Avenue East, Suite 700, Toronto, Ontario, Canada M4P 2Y3
(a division of Pearson Penguin Canada Inc.)
Penguin Ireland, 25 St Stephen's Green, Dublin 2, Ireland (a division of Penguin Books Ltd)
Penguin Group (Australia), 707 Collins Street, Melbourne, Victoria 3008, Australia
(a division of Pearson Australia Group Pty Ltd)
Penguin Books India Pvt Ltd, 11 Community Centre, Panchsheel Park, New Delhi – 110 017, India
Penguin Group (NZ), 67 Apollo Drive, Rosedale, Auckland 0632, New Zealand
(a division of Pearson New Zealand Ltd)
Penguin Books (South Africa) (Pty) Ltd, Block D, Rosebank Office Park, 181 Jan Smuts Avenue, Parktown North, Gauteng 2193, South Africa

Penguin Books Ltd, Registered Offices: 80 Strand, London WC2R 0RL, England

puffinbooks.com

First published 2013

001

Written by Jonathan Green, Steve Cleverley and Megan Bell
Text and illustrations copyright © Mind Candy Ltd, 2013
Moshi Monsters is a trademark of Mind Candy Ltd. All rights reserved
The moral right of the author and illustrator has been asserted

Printed in China by Leo Paper Products Ltd

British Library Cataloguing in Publication Data
A CIP catalogue record for this book is available from the British Library

ISBN: 978-1-40939-272-9

MOSHIPEDIA

Can you tell the difference between a Mystic Moggy and a Pretty Kitty? Do you know where you can find Acrobatic SeaStars or Unlucky Larrikins in the wild? And what about the Games Starcade or EN-GEN – where are they?

Well, have no fear, you now have all this information at your fingertips, along with loads more. This Moshipedia is an A-Z guide to many of the delights found in Monstro City and beyond!

So what are you waiting for? Turn the page and delve in. From Aarrr! Pirate Flag to Zoshlings, it's time to learn your A to Z!

Aa-Zz

Aa

Aarrr! Pirate Flag

Display this flag and support the Pirates Against Raw Treatment Yaargh.

Abominable Snow Furi

Legends say that a great beast of a Furi wanders the icy plains of Frosty Pop Glacier, searching for snacks to fill his ever-grumbling stomach.

Agony Ant

A gaggle of Woolly Blue Hoodoos and a few Furry Heebees taught Agony Ant everything they know about fortune telling up in Hokery Pokery Heights. Now she regularly graces the pages of *The Daily Growl* to bestow her wisdom on its readers.

Angel - *The SkyPony*

Until recently, SkyPonies were mentioned only in Moshi legend. But that was before a whole herd appeared, as if by magic, on a pink cloud, high above Mount Sillimanjaro. These heavenly creatures rarely visit ground level, but when they do they tell tales of a strange world in the sky where everything is soft and fluffy.

Art Lee

Art Lee is an amateur graffiti artist, working towards being Monstro City's next Danksy. Art spends his time in the Underground Caves, creating super-sweet works of pop art and is well known for being able to eat spider lollies in one bite.

Arties

Is your favourite place to hang out in Moshi world the Googenheim Gallery? Think you know your Roarbrandt from your Picarrgghhso? Do you love the smell of oil paint in the morning? Then these art-obsessed Moshlings are for you. Just don't expect your house to stay clean. After all, you can't make great art without making a great mess!

Bb

A
B
C
D
E
F
G
H
I
J
K
L
M
N
O
P
Q
R
S
T
U
V
W
X
Y
Z

Babs

Babs has sold thousands of rare and extraordinary items to citizens of Monstro City. She credits her perfect hair to the Sneeze Wax Company, insisting that floor wax contains perfect conditioning properties.

Babs' Boutique

Babs was the first merchant to open a shop at The Port. It's here that you can buy collectibles for your monster's room, including WallScrawls and Beanie Blobs.

Bacon Lounger

Mmmmm . . . bacon. That's what you'll say when you sit in this extra crispy salt-cured chair.

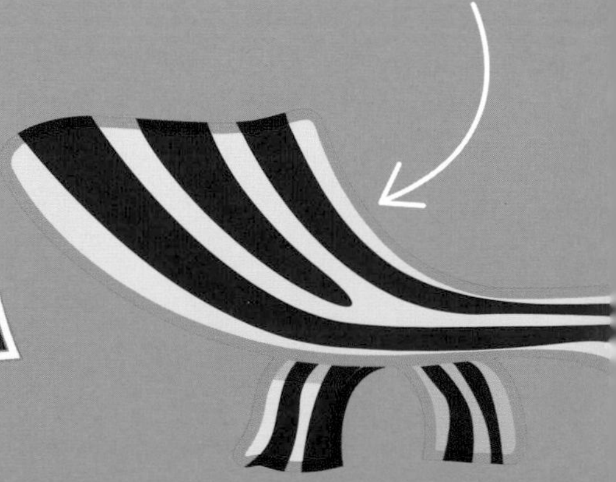

The Baddielac 9000

Dr. Strangeglove's wicked new ride that's loaded with extras – everything from the Self-Destruct-O-Matic (that causes the BaddieLac 9000 to explode into squillions of goo-splattered bits, rather than fall into Super Moshi hands!) and the Deluxe Ear Whacker 2078 Sound System (that blasts out scary organ music and allows Dr. Strangeglove to listen to his), to the Boingtastic Ejector Seat (that boings Dr. Strangeglove out of harm's way when he needs to make a super-fast escape) and the Terrible Tailfins (purely decorative, but they look really mean). And don't forget the Goo Boosters, the Fire-Breathing Gloop Spreader, C.L.O.N.C.-tastic Extendable Hub Caps, the Quad-Atomic-Goo-injected jet engine, the hidden Glump-blasters . . .

Bangers and Mash

New high-explosive variety. The big bang method of cooking potatoes.

Barfalona Chair

A super stylish chair and only slightly sticky. Eeeww!

Barfmallows

Super sticky with just a hint of icky. New from Dastardly Delights!

Barmy Swami Jungle

In the lush green depth of the Barmy Swami Jungle you'll find Snuggly Tiger Cubs like Jeepers sharpening their claws and licking old swoonafish cans.

Bass Drum and Tom Toms

Put the pedal to the metal and throw out a ferocious backbeat. Hit it!

Bat Mobile

A good decoration for bright days or dark knights. (Robin not included.)

Baz Barnacle

Who sells seashells on the seashore? Baz does! Scoffing sand makes perfect sense to Baz Barnacle. That's 'cos he spends too long lazing in the sun, swallowing sea water and partying with his best mate, Bonzer the Prawn! When he's not snoozing or surfing, Baz loves barbecuing sandcastles outside his shack, where he sells stuff that he, er ... 'borrows' from his cousin Cap'n Buck. Aaarrrr!

Beanie Blobs

Bounce your way over to buy these bloomin' brilliant Beanie Blobs! Can you collect them all?

Beasties

The Beasties are wild Moshlings — and by wild we don't mean they like to party all night! There are ticklish Tiger Cubs, lazy Hickopotumuses, Fiery Frazzledragons and even pixel-allergic Pandas. Most Moshlingologists believe the Beasties are descended from those Jurassic geriatrics the Sillysauruses — which must mean they're related to Dinos! (Just don't go telling the Beasties that.)

Beau Squiddly

Beau Squiddly is a local jazz musician named one of Monstro City's best new artists. After several platinum albums and a few number one hits, he lost his fortune to excess and a caviar obsession that keeps him fishing to this day.

A
B
C
D
E
F
G
H
I
J
K
L
M
N
O
P
Q
R
S
T
U
V
W
X
Y
Z

Betty - *The Yodelling MooMoo*

"Yodel-ay-hee-mooooo!" Next time you hear that unmistakable call you'll know that a Yodelling MooMoo is close by. But not that close because these opera-trained Moshlings can be heard from miles away. In fact their yodelling is so loud it's often used to trigger avalanches.

Bentley - *The Supah Loofah*

Once used as back scrubbers by rich Monsters, Supah Loofahs are the helpful little Moshlings that can hold half an ocean's worth of water in their squishy bodies. And that's just as well 'cos if they stay in the sun for too long they can dry out and crumble to bits.

Bert

Bert is the shyest worker at Gift Island and just hates to be disturbed. He always keeps one eye on the water and believes the stories about giant monster-munching jelly fuzzes – maybe that's why he's sweating so much.

A
B
C
D
E
F
G
H
I
J
K
L
M
N
O
P
Q
R
S
T
U
V
W
X
Y
Z

Big Bad Bill - *The Woolly Blue Hoodoo*

Woolly Blue Hoodoos are wise old Moshlings who know everything about lotions, potions, hexes and spells. If you've got a pain in the rear or a bug in your ear, these helpful furballs will cure it before you can say "umba-wanga-thlunk". Maybe even faster. Never seen without their mystical Staffs of Power, Woolly Blue Hoodoos are not as brave as most of their patients – they're scared of teaspoons! Big Bad Bill's travels took him from the sweltering Gombala Gombala Jungle to the Moshi Monsters' first album *Music Rox*! He and the Woolly Blue Hoodoos breakthrough track was 'Go Do The Hoodoo'.

Big Bad Boombox

Click it on to crank up the tunes while you're decorating your house, or just to dance! (Available in Pomegranate Pink or Blueberry Blue.)

Big Chief Tiny Head

This greedy, Bongo Colada-slurping baddie has been desperate to restore his itty-bitty bonce to its former glory ever since a Woolly Blue Hoodoo shrank it in an argument over fried Oobla Doobla!

A
B
C
D
E
F
G
H
I
J
K
L
M
N
O
P
Q
R
S
T
U
V
W
X
Y
Z

Big Earl

Big Earl is a big plant with big attitude. Put him in your room and scare away all your visitors.

Big Enid

Big Earl's wife. Just as big, twice as scary.

Billy Bob Baitman

Giving it his all for a fisherman's haul, Billy Bob Baitman could do with a few tips because the only thing he's caught lately is an old boot. Billy Bob is still fishing for the other boot to make a matched pair.

Bird's Nest

Twit twoo twit twoo! That's Birdish for "Cool Nest", donchaknow?

A
B
C
D
E
F
G
H
I
J
K
L
M
N
O
P
Q
R
S
T
U
V
W
X
Y
Z

Birdies

From deck-spinning Disco Duckies to bookish Owls of Wiseness, the Birdie Moshlings have little in common except for wings and beaks - Stunt Penguins can't even fly!

Bizarre Bazaar

The Bizarre Bazaar really lives up to its name, for here you can buy such exotic items as a Shark in a Bowl and dinosaur parts! These curious treasures have been brought back from the Arctic wastelands of the Yappalatian Mountains by Bushy Fandango, who explores the snowy wilderness guided by her team of trusty Musky Huskies.

Bjorn Squish

With an appetite for construction, Roarker Bjorn Squish is always on lunch break. By promising to bring extra sandwiches to work, he's gained special permission from his supervisor, Dizzee Bolt, to eat and eat the whole day through.

Black Jack

Mad, bad and dangerous to know, Black Jack is one mean Glump. Even other Glumps steer clear of this fearsome ball of fury – especially if he's knocking down the citizens of Monstro City with a Cannonball Cavalcade!

Blakey Hollow

Here's where you'll find Bustling Buslings taking the weight off, relaxing on little piles of bricks.

Bleurgh Lagoon

The coral reef of Bleurgh Lagoon is the natural habitat of the energetic Acrobatic SeaStars.

Blingo - *The Flashy Fox*

Slick, cool and super funky, Flashy Foxes never take off their shades. That's not because it's sunny up in Hipsta Hills, it's to avoid the glare of their gleaming bling! When these hip little Moshlings are not listening to the latest tunes on their superfly boomboxes, they enjoy hanging out in Horrods and making up silly rhymes in their strange, lightning-fast language. Udigwotsgoindown?

Blinki
- *The All-Seeing Moment Muncher*

With his long-range Moshiscopic eye, nifty side-jets and twiddly transmitter, Blinki is fully equipped to capture any moment, no matter how bizarre. And that's just as well because this adventure-seeking Moshling is Roary Scrawl's Moshi-cam partner in movie-making magic. Blinki can even play back the moments he munches via his holographic projector.

Blitzin' Blender

Blend this, blend that, blend your furniture, just DON'T blend your monster.

Blobert

Green and gooey, fun but just a little bit screwy – that's your new pal Blobert! He's a funny green splodge, but give him a tickle and he'll entertain you by changing shape as only Blobert can.

Bloopy

Bloopy is feeling blue, but so would you if you had a face like a squished blueberry! Anyway, don't take pity because this badly-behaved blob loves splatting Moshlings with Mega Glump Thumps. Ouch!

A
B
C
D
E
F
G
H
I
J
K
L
M
N
O
P
Q
R
S
T
U
V
W
X
Y
Z

Bobbi SingSong
- The Jollywood Singaling

If you've never been to Jollywood (it is jolly good) chances are you've no idea how famous Bobbi SingSong really is. A legend in his distant homeland, this Moshling gooperstar's smash hit 'Welcome to Jollywood' was even adopted as Jollywood's national anthem. If only he could remember his mantra!

Blurp - *The Batty Bubblefish*

All puffed-up with nowhere to blow, Batty Bubblefish spend most days swimming around in circles holding their breath. These sub-aquatic Moshlings have got such terrible memories they can't remember what it is they're supposed to have forgotten. Make sure to avoid upsetting one as they can splurt out gallons of multi-coloured gloop.

A B C D E F G H I J K L M N O P Q R S T U V W X Y Z

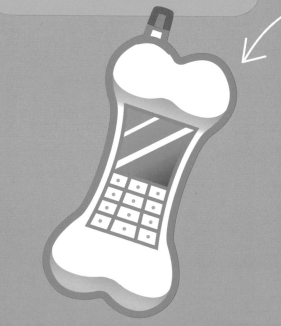

Bodge - *The Artful Splodger*

Why do a job properly when you can bodge it? Why indeed because Artful Splodgers are the messy Moshlings that just love slopping paint all over the place. When they are not attempting to decorate Moshi houses, these playful paint pots enjoy creating foot paintings of famous monsters. Look out, wet paint!

Bone Phone

Phoney Bone Phones may Drone: Own a Known Bone Phone.

Bongo Colada

Sip it all up with CocoLoco's tasty head full of Bongo Colada! Slurp, BURP!

Bonkers

Possibly the only one of his kind, Bonkers has learned to perform acrobatic tricks to make enough Rox for his rent at Sludgetown Apartments. Bonkers' favourite food is Pop Rox.

Boomer - *The Bigmouth Squiddly Dee*

Stuff your ears with cotton wool – Bigmouth Squiddly Dees are seriously loud. They might look all fluffy and harmless, but every time you touch one it opens its gigantic cakehole and yells like a foghorn. What's with the bandage? It's actually loo roll that they wrap around their fluffy heads to protect their ears from their own blaring shrieks.

A
B
C
D
E
F
G
H
I
J
K
L
M
N
O
P
Q
R
S
T
U
V
W
X
Y
Z

Brain BonBons

Brain BonBons are infused with neuron-tingling gooey centres. Known to improve culinary IQ, these are Zommer's favourites.

Breakfast Bayou

Discovered by Cap'n Buck, this toasty isle is always sunny side up. You can lounge about on the Sausage Sofa or sizzle the day away on the Bacon Lounger.

Bruiser

Cheer up Bruiser, you look like you've been dragged through a hedge backwards. What's that? You have? Oh dear, it's probably because you can't help causing mayhem with your Scarface Smashes and Scowling ScrimScrams.

Bubba's Brother

Bubba's Brother is the twin brother of Bubba the Bouncer and Zack Binspin's personal bodyguard. You can tell him and his brother apart because he has a scar above his left eye, whereas Bubba has a scar above his right eye. Simple when you know how!

Bubble Blowin' Puzzle

Gather the pieces and put them together to reveal a funny monster scene.

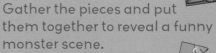

Bubba

Bubba is a prominent tattoo artist and nightclub bouncer. He works at the Underground Disco and practises his moves at home on his Dance, Dance, Roarvolution machine. He hopes to show off his style in an upcoming dance-off, if he ever gets a day off.

Bug Juice

Squeezed on the fly for extra bug!

Bug 'n' Ratty

Bug 'n' Ratty, or Ratty 'n' Bug as Ratty would insist, are ALWAYS up to some sort of mischief. Whether it's rearranging dino bones over at the Unnatural History Museum or stealing Pepperbombs from the Pepperbomb Geyser ... you'll always find them up to no good.

Build-a-Bot

Collect the bits to build your very own robotic chum. Just don't leave him out in the rain to rust.

Bug's Big Bounce

Bounce your way to the top of Monstro City and beyond! How high can you make Bug bounce? Buy your own Big Bounce arcade game at the Games Starcade and find out!

BUG'S BIG BOUNCE

Bumblechops Manor

One of Buster Bumblechops' homes, built with the aid of a gang of Titchy TrundleBots.

Burnie - *The Fiery Frazzledragon*

These cheeky flying Beasties get into all kinds of sizzly mayhem, especially if they've been guzzling gasoline. It's their favourite drink, but it gives them terrible flaming hiccups. Stand back or you might get toasted! Rumour has it that Fiery Frazzledragons were once employed by Super Moshis to heat up cauldrons of dew stew and char-grill silly sausages. Hiccup!

Bushy Fandango

Bushy Fandango vacations in the sub-zero temperatures of the Yappalation Mountains. Guided by her team of trusty Musky Husky puppies, she explores the snowy wilds, occasionally encountering an Abominable Furi and bringing treasures back to the Bizarre Bazaar.

A
B
C
D
E
F
G
H
I
J
K
L
M
N
O
P
Q
R
S
T
U
V
W
X
Y
Z

Busling - *The Bustling Busling*

The wheels on the bus go round and round? You bet they do! Bustling Buslings are the automated Moshlings that tootle around the world of Moshi, stopping every now and then to . . . erm, well they can't pick up any passengers because they are too titchy. Stick out your arm and one might just pull over for a chat.

Buster Bumblechops

Buster Bumblechops is Monstro City's own Moshling collector extraordinaire. Whether it's Puppies, Worldies, or Fluffies you're after, Buster Bumblechops has the Moshling hints and tips for you!

Cadabra Flash

Cadabra Flash is a gleaming light formation near the Crazy Canyons where you'll find Performing Flappasauruses enjoying life in its glare.

Cake House

Thanks to the Gingerbread School of Architecture, you can now have your cake and live in it! You can buy this mouth-watering biscuit-based building from the New Houses store on Ooh La Lane.

Cali - *The Valley Mermaid*

Like, wow! There's something totally fishy going on here. When Valley Mermaids are not freaking out over the latest koi band or knocking back cappuccinos at Starfishbucks, they're hooking up fellow Moshlings. In fact their hearts begin to flash whenever they sense romance. What-ever!

Candy Apple

With the ability to dislodge fully-grown fangs, the Candy Apple might bite off more than you can chew.

Candy Cane Caves

Cherry Bomb was first discovered here. There are no shops (what did you expect?), but you will find the mini game Moshi Cupcakes. Beware of the wicked Sweet Tooth though, who can often be found lurking in these candied caverns.

Candy Coral

In the sea around Candy Shoals, rare coral grows in candy form.

Candy of Ultimate Evil

Sweet Tooth's ultimate objective is to discover the secret formula needed to create the Candy of Ultimate Evil. So far the sugar-besotted rogue has failed, but ultimately . . . Who knows?

Candy Shoals

From Marshmallow Waterfalls, to Grape Gloop Geyser, Candy Shoals is a sugary paradise. It was discovered by Cap'n Buck, who thoroughly sampled its many delights . . .

Candy Standy

Stick your monster's clothes to this handy candy standy.

Candy the Scare Bear

Cute little Candy loves to play with anything pink. Watch your jewellery – she'll have it in a flash! Collect the whole set.

Cap'n Buck's Ship in a Bottle

Ahoy! Here be a mini *Cloudy Cloth Clipper* to decorate your piratey quarters.

Captain Buck E. Barnacle

Orphaned by a terrible shipwreck, Cap'n Buck was raised by a school of Batty Bubblefish in Potion Ocean. Unable to quell his sailing urges, Buck returned to a life of piracy, captaining the *Cloudy Cloth Clipper* and collecting booty from places like Bubblebath Bay and Candy Shoals.

Captain Codswallop

Captain of the *Gooey Galleon*, this crazy buccaneer was once the scourge of the Seventy Seas. Some say his facial fuzz is made from enchanted seaweed, others say it's rotten cabbage stuck on with fish paste. Either way, it stinks. Aaaaarrrr!

A
B
C
D
E
F
G
H
I
J
K
L
M
N
O
P
Q
R
S
T
U
V
W
X
Y
Z

Carter - *The Barking RahRah*

Only mad dogs and Barking RahRahs go out in the midday sun. Perhaps that explains why these sun-worshipping Moshlings enjoy shuffle-dancing in the sand and striking weird poses from ancient tomb paintings. But is a Barking RahRah's bark worse than its bite? You bet, because it sounds like a Silly Snuffler sitting on a broken kazoo.

Captain Squirk

As heroic captain of the *Rhapsody 2*, Squirk's primary objective is to explore monstery new worlds, seek out quirky new melodies, and boldly go where no Zoshling has gone before. There's more to Captain Squirk than whooshing around the stars – this multi-talented alien can play any tune in the Swooniverse on the spoons.

Carton of Sour Milk

Nutritious, healthy milk left in the sun for a few days, to 'mature'. Sounds gross, but monsters seem to like it!

A B C D E F G H I J K L M N O P Q R S T U V W X Y Z

Casper

Casper is frightened by any loud noises. He spends his days counting gifts and trying not to get distracted by visitors arriving on the nearby ferry.

Catacactus

We catch all our Catacacti in the Dreaded Dunes, tempting the prickly puss plants out with spiky cat food.

Cat Ears

Meow! Give these to your monster and they'll look like a cat. Catnip sold separately.

Cave Man and Woman (Iced)

How long have the Cave Man and Woman been frozen in ice? It's a Moshi mystery, but beware of defrosting them, they don't look too happy . . .

Ceiling Slime

Give your home that 'unlived in' look with this gloopy decor.

Chainsaw Thru Head!

Make it look like your Zommer had a mishap with a chainsaw with this gruesome hat.

Cherry Bomb - *The Baby Boomer*

Quick! Stick your fingers in your ears, the Baby Boomers are here. But don't panic, these clockwork Moshlings rarely go boom. The reason they're so noisy is because their fuses fizz and crackle whenever they're excited. Fzzzttt!

Chick Checker

Chick Checker's noisy peeps kept the whole of Monstro City awake, but with the clang and clamour of Gift Island, he found a home that none would complain about. He's famous for predicting weather changes and catching worms.

A B C D E F G H I J K L M N O P Q R S T U V W X Y Z

28

ChillyBot State Park

You'll find Titchy-Tusked Mammoths dozing in blocks of ice in ChillyBot State Park.

Chip the Scare Bear

CHIP! CHIP! He never listens, off in a world of his own, getting down to trance! Collect the whole set.

Chocolate Coated Broccoli

Worse than it sounds — and it sounds pretty bad to begin with!

Chop Chop - *The Cheeky Chimp*

As well as being part-time ninjas, Cheeky Chimps are full-time jokers. They leave a trail of whoopee cushions, banana skins and stink bombs wherever they go. In fact these playful primates just don't know when to stop. That can be pretty funny – unless the joke's on you. So watch out or you could end up with a face full of custard pie and a rubber chicken in your soup. Ha-dee-ha!

Chomper and Stomper

With an ever-present overgrowth problem in Monstro City, Chomper and Stomper have their work cut out for them. They mow the grass every day in exchange for free-range permissions from the local farmer.

Circus Cannon

BOOM! Don't stand too close, you never know when this thing'll go off.

Cirque du Moshi

Roll up! Roll up! It's the spectacular spectacular you've all been waiting for. Step right up folks, the Cirque Du Moshi is here to entertain you! Located on Music Island, it's more fun than a cream custard pie to the face. So why not stop by and play a game of Quack Attack before stepping over to the Super Moshi Merch shop to gather yourself some sweet Super Moshi gear? Nothing tops this big top!

Clearly Classical

Some people might think this style of music is as dead as the composers who first made it popular centuries ago – Moshis like Goatzart, Furi Feethoven and Raaahms – but the truth is it's the style that inspired the scores to all those blockbuster movies the Moshi Monsters love to watch at the Monstro City Googleplex.

Clem

Listening to Hop-Hop music and working on robotic donut rigs are Clem's favourite hobbies. Fortunately, Gift Island needed a RoboDonut Roarker, and Clem was the first choice for the job.

C.L.O.N.C.

Cleo - *The Pretty Pyramid*

Experts thought Pretty Pyramids were extinct until a fierce sandstorm blew away a huge desert dune to reveal the lost valley where they live and play. Apart from bathing in milk, munching on grapes and making big sandcastles, these friendly Moshlings spend their days searching for lost treasure and painting funny squiggles on walls. They also love riddles, precious stones (especially Rox) and anything made of gold.

Life isn't always a bowl of Swirlberry Muffins for the monsters of Moshi world. At times – all too frequently, in fact – the peace of Monstro City is broken by the mischievous machinations of the Criminal League Of Naughty Critters – known as C.L.O.N.C. for short. A mish-mash of felonious misfits, included among their number are the villainous Dr. Strangeglove, his Glumps, Sweet Tooth (who's mad, bad and dangerous to slurp), Frau Now BrownKau, Big Chief Tiny Head, Commander Sassafras, Biggie Diddles III and the Robo-Quacks.

The C.L.O.N.C. Star

This skull-shaped station is the hub of all C.L.O.N.C.'s inter-cosmic operations. The red light emitted by the station is visible from Monstro City's Observatory!

C.L.O.N.C. Super Weapon

Whatever will the villainous masterminds behind the Criminal League Of Naughty Critters come up with next? This giant magnifying glass carrying a C.L.O.N.C. satellite is smokin'! Agony Ant in particular should watch out!

ClothEar Cloud Formation

Scientists believe Fancy Banshees come from a parallel vortex deep within the ClothEar Cloud Formation. It can only be accessed by running around and saying 'woo-oo-oo' really loudly.

Cloud Chair

Now you can sit on Cloud 9 in the one and only Cloud Chair. Lightning bolt footstool not included.

A
B
C
D
E
F
G
H
I
J
K
L
M
N
O
P
Q
R
S
T
U
V
W
X
Y
Z

Cloudy Cloth Clipper

The *Cloudy Cloth Clipper* has everything a barnacle-encrusted old pirate like Cap'n Buck E. Barnacle could want, including a big red main mast, a mizzen, a rudder, a captain's cabin and a poop deck. (Well, you never know when you might get caught short at sea.)

Cluekoo

Even green-thumbed monsters need a little help sometimes, so thankfully there's the Cluekoo who lives in your Moshling Garden. The Cluekoo watches everything that goes on when you're not there and will tell you if any little Moshlings have stopped by for a nibble.

Clutch

Clutch has been delivering gifts from Gift Island for almost thirty years. Well past the point of retiring, his love for smiling monster owners keeps him coming back day after day.

Cobweb

Make your room look decrepit with cobwebs taken straight from the scariest place in Monstro City – under Roary Scrawl's sofa!

A
B
C
D
E
F
G
H
I
J
K
L
M
N
O
P
Q
R
S
T
U
V
W
X
Y
Z

CocoLoco - *The Naughty Nutter*

Fancy a drink? You're in good company because Naughty Nutters can't stop sipping Bongo Colada from their nutty heads. It's refreshing stuff but it makes them slightly nuts – conga-ing, limbo-ing and partying the night away. Crazier still, they love shaking their maracas whilst bossanova-ing over breakfast!

Colonel Catcher

Obsessed with pinning Flutterby species to his Genus of Monstro City whiteboard, Colonel Catcher retired early from his tour of Bendia, and can be found roaming Flutterby Field with shouts of exasperation as he tries to catch new beauties.

Colorama

If you want to give your Moshi Monster a makeover, then get yourself down to the Colorama. It's here that you can change the colour of your monster's body, boots and even their eyes using the Colorizer machine!

A
B
C
D
E
F
G
H
I
J
K
L
M
N
O
P
Q
R
S
T
U
V
W
X
Y
Z

The Contraption

It whirrs, it spins, but what does it actually do? No one knows, but it sure looks cool!

Commander Sassafras

NOW HEAR THIS! Raging mad and power crazy, Commander Sassafras is the seething buffoon responsible for C.L.O.N.C.'s military strategy. When he's not losing his temper, foaming at the mouth and SHOUTING REALLY LOUDLY, this red-faced rascal can be found shuffling toy glumps around his Campaign table and polishing his pretend medals.

Cookie Stacker

Build your own Leaning Tower of Cookies. Be careful not to eat from the bottom!

A
B
C
D
E
F
G
H
I
J
K
L
M
N
O
P
Q
R
S
T
U
V
W
X
Y
Z

Coolio - *The Magical Sparklepop*

It sounds a trifle absurd but these tubby Moshlings are enchanted. Whenever they need to chill, glittery sparks zing around their slurpy swirls accompanied by jingly-jangly nursery rhymes. This happens quite a lot because Magical Sparklepops go all gloopy if they get too hot. But what's with the funny waddle? Well, you try walking wearing a wafery tub!

Cosmic Gloop

Used for lubricating all kinds of Zoshling contraptions. This icky stuff also has magical auto-tuning properties. Just one teaspoon a day and you'll be giving Missy Kix a run for her Rox!

Cosmo - *The Mini Moshulator*

Able to calculate the cost of a billion gooberries in seconds, Mini Moshulators are the friendly Moshlings you can count on – literally because they love having their buttons pushed. Press 'em in a certain order and they might even hand you a printout of a popular equation and beep a fraction of a tune.

Crazy Bad Bill

Crazy Bad Bill is a Woolly Orange HooDoo. His pet croc Dundee likes Oobla Doobla, and he lives in Snaggletooth Swamp.

Crazy Caves of Fang-Ten Valley

Home to the Furry Heebees where you'll find the batty biters hanging out – upside-down!

Crazy Daisy

Use this Super Seed as part of a combo to catch ShiShi or I.G.G.Y. and more!

Creepy Crawler

Perfect for green-fingered monsters. Make sure you keep it pruned, or you may find your monster all tied up in the morning.

A
B
C
D
E
F
G
H
I
J
K
L
M
N
O
P
Q
R
S
T
U
V
W
X
Y
Z

Crispy Bat Wings

Sonar-fried for extra crunch, these tasty monster treats are perfect for lunch. Or breakfast, or dinner, or a late-night snack . . .

Crystal Chandelier

You'll be the talk of the town with this masterpiece shimmering away in your room.

Cuddly Human

Just what every monster needs – their very own human to cuddle in bed. This one's a squishy little businessman!

Cry Baby

Cry Baby could leave his barred prison in the Underground Tunnels any time he wishes, but he loves attention from monster owners and waits there daily to give another howling cry. He's only in the first grade – give him a break!

A
B
C
D
E
F
G
H
I
J
K
L
M
N
O
P
Q
R
S
T
U
V
W
X
Y
Z

Cuddly Pirate

Avast, me hearties!
Splice the main
brace! Give me
a cuddle!
Aarrr!

Cup O Gruel

The most gruelling food in the
Gross-ery Store!

Cutie Pie - *The Wheelie Yum Yum*

Check out the wheels! These
scrumptilicious Moshlings move
like lightning, but so would you if
you had turbo-charged sprinkles
and a woowoo-ing cherry on your
head. Wheelie YumYums are often
forced to flee from hungry predators,
leaving spongy crumbs in their wake.
Follow the trail and you might find
one filling up with a few gallons of
super sweet cocoa.

Dd

Daily Growl

The Daily Growl

The Daily Growl is the Moshi newspaper. If there's anything going on in Monstro City, you can bet that editor-in-chief Roary Scrawl and his team of roving reporters will know about it. And soon they will be breaking the news across the Moshi world – whether it's about a Moshling stuck up a tree or news of Dr. Strangeglove's latest wicked scheme!

Dewy

Dewy is a real DIY kind of guy. He once constructed a jet-powered jelly bean sorter out of a plastic fork, Bangers and Mash, a rubber band, and a Plank. He loves flipping through back issues of *Hammer Times* and getting brain freezes from Slug Slurp Slushies.

Diavlos

When Diavlos are happy they're fangtastically cheeky, but bug them too much and they become fiery and sneaky! Maybe it's all that sizzly-fizzly lava in their cratery heads? Yow!

Diavlo's Duds

Owned by a fiery red and coal-black Diavlo, funnily enough, Diavlo's Duds sells small clothes – mostly made for Diavlos, funnily enough – although it does stock some other kinds of clothing, too. Lots of Diavlos like to shop there, funnily enough, for cool stuff, funnily en— Hang on! *Cool* stuff? Diavlos? Those volcanic little hotheads?

'Diggin' Ya Lingo!'

If you think Blingo's lightning-fast rapping is monsterific you'll be blown away by his first solo track, 'Diggin' Ya Lingo!'

Dime Mine

You'll find Mini Moneys like Penny deep inside the shiny Dime Mine.

Dinos

These reptilian rascals have been roaming the Moshi world since forever. They have incredibly small brains, making them as slow on the uptake as continental drift. They have a perfectly understandable fear of enormous asteroids and a not-quite-so-understandable fear of rubber spears.

Dipsy - *The Dinky Dreamcloud*

Dinky Dreamclouds dream of one day becoming Ginormous Dreamclouds, but they are far too teeny for that important job. Instead they flutter and flap about all day making cute noises and admiring their eyelashes. Don't get them angry – they might rain on you!

Disco Lights

D-d-d-dance eveeerrrryboodyyy! Rock the house with these disco lights.

Diver's Fishtank

You might want to watch your fingers with this surprising tank. Put it in your room, click it, and see what happens!

The DIY Shop

Located on Sludge Street, the Do It Yourself Shop is run by the messy monster Dewy. The DIY shop is particularly known for its handy objects, stunning wallpaper, crazy doors and elegant floor choices.

Dizzee Bolt

Maintaining the nuts and bolts of the EN-GEN system is tough work for Dizzee Bolt, who takes pride in her hard hat and coveralls. Monstro City's Chief EN-GENeer's hobbies include knitting, weight- lifting, sludge sizzling and roar-b-q parties.

DJ Quack - *The Disco Duckie*

You can tell by the way they waddle that Disco Duckies were born to boogie. When they're not flapping around mirrorballs and dipping their beaks in glittery gloop, these music-mad Moshlings are busy busting out new dance moves and slicking back their feathers with orange sauce. If you ever meet one in a dark alley, be sure to duck – they can't see a thing with those shades on. Quack!

'Do the Doodle!'

'Do the Doodle' is Mr. Snoodle's first ever video release, and it's totally roarsome! We would say it's his first song, but Mr. Snoodle doesn't sing – he just parps! That said, the Silly Snuffler's 'Do the Doodle' dance has taken Monstro City by storm! In the video Mr. Snoodle's doodling takes him under the sea, off Moshi world to the Moon, and even into a video game. Radically retro!

'The Doctor Will See You Now'

'The Doctor Will See You Now' is the track Dr. Strangeglove and the Glump Generation recorded for Simon Growl's *Music Rox* album. When this tune starts rocking, Musky Huskies better beware!

Dodgy Dealz

Dodgy Dealz is a shop on Sludge Street, run by the shady, tentacled dealer Sly Chance. He will happily take any food or furniture that you don't need off your hands. The shop is also home to Ratty, the three-eyed rat.

WEEVIL KNEEVIL'S DOWNHILL DASH

7560

Downhill Dash

Grab your stunt bike and collect as many stars as you can in this high speed, downhill dash. Buy your own Downhill Dash arcade game at the Games Starcade!

Doris - *The Rummaging Plotamus*

Unlike regular Plotamuses, Rummaging Plotamuses are obsessed with digging for fluffles – valuable toadstools that smell of liquorice. These gentle little Moshlings then knit the fluffles into nests which they hibernate in for much of the year. When they're not burrowing or snoozing, Plotamuses love gardening (well, digging up dirt) and gossiping about celebrities. And that's what makes them ideal pets – as long as you're not famous. You dig?

Dr. C. Fingz

Able to read minds via his telepathic wiggle-stalk, Dr. C. Fingz is the *Rhapsody 2*'s chief medical officer. When he's not bandaging up battered Zoshlings, this fuzzy fella uses his powers to communicate with alien beings across the Swooniverse. The good doctor can even temporarily extract talent from other critters, so one minute he can move like Bobbi SingSong, the next he can sing like Zack Binspin.

Dorothy's Shoes

Now click your heels and say, "There's No Place Like Monstro City!"

46

Dr. Furbert Snufflepeeps

Dr. Snufflepeeps is the legendary Moshlingologist who taught both Younger Furi and Lavender Troggs when they were at Super Moshiversity.

Dr. Strangeglove

Cropping up here, there and everywhere, Dr. Strangeglove is a scientific genius and former Doctor of Moshlingology who served as a Sinister Minister in the gloomy days of the Glunge Age. Strangeglove developed a twisted hatred for Moshlings after a Musky Husky he was experimenting on mistook his hand for a packet of sausages and mangled it – thus the glove. His favourite pastime is glumping Moshlings and wreaking mayhem. He's not a fan of Musky Huskies or bad trombonists.

Dragon Fruit

Grow these special seeds in your Moshling Garden and you'll soon have tasty Dragon Fruit springing up all over the place! Dragon Fruit are what you need if you want to attract ShiShi, Hansel, Fifi, Purdy, DJ Quack or Prof. Purplex to your garden.

DRAGON FRUIT

A
B
C
D
E
F
G
H
I
J
K
L
M
N
O
P
Q
R
S
T
U
V
W
X
Y
Z

Dream Snatcher

This mystical item can make your dreams twist and turn with the wind, taking you to places you never knew existed, if you can find it.

Drool Metal

Drool Metal is the new-old musical style that will take you to metal heaven. Characterised by heavily distorted guitar, tremolo picking, blast beat drumming and deep growling vocals, it's the heavy rock sound that's been made popular all over again by rising gooperstar Zommer. You don't need to be able to remove your own arm and use it as a drumstick, of course, but what can you say . . . it helps!

Dundee

Dundee is Crazy Bad Bill's pink pet croc-monster. He likes nothing better than chomping on Oobla Doobla while sunning himself in Snaggletooth Swamp.

Duster of Destiny

One of the rarest and most mysterious items found in the shops of Monstro City. What does it do? Only one way to find out!

A
B
C
D
E
F
G
H
I
J
K
L
M
N
O
P
Q
R
S
T
U
V
W
X
Y
Z

Ee

Easter Bunny Ears

Big bunny ears can help your monster listen out for hidden Easter eggs.

Easter Bunny Cuddly Human

A cuddly bunny ... no wait, it's a human dressed as a bunny. Double cute!

Ecto - *The Fancy Banshee*

Don't be afraid, Fancy Banshees are among the friendliest Moshlings of all. Don't touch one – their creepy glowing capes are made of electrified wobble-plasma. This mysterious stuff turns things inside-out. Eek! When they're not drifting through walls in the dead of night, these totally silent, super-rare Moshlings float around collecting Rox dust. No one knows why, but it's thought they need to absorb it to keep glowing.

A
B
C
D
E
F
G
H
I
J
K
L
M
N
O
P
Q
R
S
T
U
V
W
X
Y
Z

Eggplant

A plant with eggs. What were you expecting?

Egon Groanay

He's the biggest critic in Monstro City, soooo undercover, you've probably never heard of him. From Garlic Marshmallows to the Pants of Power, he's reviewed them all. Constantly checking for new releases in *The Daily Growl*, Egon Groanay makes sure all our stock is tip-top.

Egyptian Cat Statue

This super-rare Egyptian Cat Statue will look great in your tomb, err ... room.

Elder Furi

If it's guidance you seek, look no further because Elder Furi is the all-seeing, all-knowing leader of the Super Moshis. He might seem a bit old and crusty, but this ultra-powerful monster knows everything there is to know about ... well, everything. How? Rumour has it he tumbled into the mythical Well of Wisdom as a baby and emerged chanting 'Ohmmmmm!' through his flowing beard.

A B C D E F G H I J K L M N O P Q R S T U V W X Y Z

Elmore the Great

Elmore wasn't always so great. The biggest monster in Monstro City, he once tripped and fell, blocking the Grub Truck from getting to Monstro City, and making for some very hungry monsters. Everyone worked together to get Elmore out of a pickle and then celebrated with a new holiday – Growly Grub Day!

EN-GEN

EN-GEN provides Monstro City with all of its energy, pumping out Monstrowatts day and night. Give Dizzee Bolt a hand producing some power and you can earn yourself Rox at the same time.

Elwood

Elwood suffers several concussions a week as he is constantly striking himself in the face with his spade. Unfortunately, due to subsequent memory loss, he forgets about the dangers of standing on the handle and continues to be struck.

Essence of Blue

Squeezed from the bluest berries on the bluest bushes in the bluest part of Monstro City.

A
B
C
D
E
F
G
H
I
J
K
L
M
N
O
P
Q
R
S
T
U
V
W
X
Y
Z

Evil Sock Puppet

Wuhahaha! I am Ze Evil Sock Puppet. You'll never catch me!

Eye Phone

Using the latest technology, this super hi-tech phone is totally way ahead of its time. A must for tech-savvy monsters, just make sure you don't poke it!

Eye Pie

The tasty snack that stares back! Available from the Gross-ery Store it's very popular – blink and you'll miss it!

Eye TV

A goggle-box, for goggling at. Just hope it doesn't blink at a crucial moment!

Eyescream Sundae

Like Roarberry Cheesecake, but with half the decibels. This chilly treat makes a great morning snack!

Ff

Fabio

Capable of chomping up enemies in seconds with a Triple Tooth TerrorBite, this dim-witted Glump is interested in only two things: eating and perfecting that silly pink quiff. Fabio has even tried eating his teeth, but they tasted glumpy.

Fablo Fiasco

What a beautiful fiasco! Click on it and see how all of the pieces fall higgledy-piggledy out of place.

Fango Mandango

The dancing fruit. *Olé!*

Father Twistmas

A mysterious character, he visits Moshi world once a year, on Twistmas Eve, to deliver presents to all good little Moshlings and their monsters. His wife is Mother Twistmas. Just make sure you're on his 'Nice' list.

A
B
C
D
E
F
G
H
I
J
K
L
M
N
O
P
Q
R
S
T
U
V
W
X
Y
Z

Ferocifer

Fire up your Diavlo with this smokin' headgear!

Fingerless Gloves

Perfect for a fingerless monster!

Fifi - *The Oochie Poochie*

Ooh la la! Oochie Poochies are sweet, fluffy and totally obsessed with the finer things in life, from fancy food to the very latest fur-styles. They love getting their fluffy bits trimmed and pampered. When they're not sipping vintage lemonade or collecting designer hair clips, these snooty little Moshlings like nibbling on the yummy cotton candy they keep on the end of their tails. Scrumptious, darling!

First Officer Ooze

Always in demand thanks to the Cosmic Gloop he generates, First Officer Ooze is second in command aboard the *Rhapsody 2*. But what's with the Gloop? Well, besides lubricating all kinds of Zoshi contraptions, this icky stuff has magical auto-tuning properties – a teaspoon a day and you'll be singing like Missy Kix in no time.

A B C D E F G H I J K L M N O P Q R S T U V W X Y Z

54

Fishies

Ever seen a Bubblefish ready to blow, or a somersaulting SeaStar cartwheeling across the seabed? What about a mermaid waving at a surfing SeaHorse? You will if you ever meet these marine Moshlings!

Fishlips

With lips like that, Fishlips should have been a singer. Sadly this one-eyed blob of badness can't sing because those luscious lips are permanently sealed with gloop – perfect for delivering Suctiony Smackeroos. Yuck!

Fizzy - *The Lipsmacking Bubbly*

Thirsty? You'd better be careful if a Lipsmacking Bubbly offers you a drink – these madcap Moshlings are fizzy beyond belief. In fact, the bendy straw poking out of every Bubbly's lid is not just for sipping, it also allows the gas from all that fizzy-wizzy pop to escape so that it doesn't blow its top.

Fishy Fountain

Click on it for some seriously soothing sounds. It's sure to make a splash, and it smells better than you'd think!

A
B
C
D
E
F
G
H
I
J
K
L
M
N
O
P
Q
R
S
T
U
V
W
X
Y
Z

A
B
C
D
E
F
G
H
I
J
K
L
M
N
O
P
Q
R
S
T
U
V
W
X
Y
Z

Flumpy - *The Pluff*

Monsters often say that Pluffs are the most chilled out of all the Moshlings. It's hard to disagree when you see them strolling through the Cotton Clump plantation, arms dangling at their sides, huge grins on their faces, with not a care in the world.

Flowering Clock

Plucked from the Numeracinth Plant, Nature's own timekeeper.

Fluffies

Cuddly-wuddly and oh so snuggly, Fluffies are soft, and squishy, and incredibly cute. But be warned – they might look like the most gorgeous snuggle-soft snookums but that fluffy exterior can hide a terrible temper – and some of 'em even bite!

Flutterby Cabinet

A delicate little cabinet for showing off all your most prized possessions.

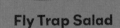

Fly Trap Salad

Be warned – it bites back!

Flying V Guitar

The Flying V Guitar is THE best way to shred your way to fame. Hey, it's worked for other Moshi bands! And turn it up to eleven with the Roarshall Speakers.

Flutterby Field

Over in Flutterby Field you can net Flutterbies in return for Rox! How handy is that? Say hi to Colonel Catcher while you are there!

Foodies

If you've got a healthy appetite, or you're feeling a bit peckish, then the Foodies are for you. With Sweet Ringy Thingies, Psycho Gingerboys, vrooming cupcakes and Magical Sparklepop ices, you'll be spoilt for choice by their sweet candy confections.

Frau Now BrownKau

Wanted in connection with gloop theft and Sandy Drain sabotage, Frau Now BrownKau is the menacing moo with friends in all the wrong places. Little is known about this former commandant of the Scary Dairy, but rumour has it her udderly fearsome false teeth are a direct result of grazing on too many grassy gobstoppers back home in StrudelHofen when she was a calf. She likes grass goolash and her vintage MooCow 4000 Milk Float, but can't stand cattle grids.

Foot Table

Now made with real feet!

Freakface

This greenish globbish Glump must have graduated with honours from the School of Drool because it can't stop dribbling. Not that manners matter – Freakface is a master of the Burbling Gurgling Gobstopper. Yeew, slimy!

Fried Egg Rug

It's so hot in here you could fry an egg on the floor. Or buy our pre-fried one!

Freaky Fossil

Just say it, don't spray it! This Freaky Fossil has some real attitude. Click it and see!

A B C D E F G H I J K L M N O P Q R S T U V W X Y Z

Fumble - *The Acrobatic SeaStar*

Gimme five! When they're not boinging along the seabed performing death-defying stunts or bungee-ing from towering coral formations, Acrobatic SeaStars spend most days gluing their pointy bits back on. And that's because they're a bit accident-prone. In fact they're the clumsiest Moshlings in town. Thing is, they can't resist showing-off, even if it means tumbling face-first into a pile of poisonous seagrass. Now that's gotta hurt!

Frosty Pop Glacier

The Frosty Pop Glacier is a wintry wonderland near Potion Ocean where you'll find the likes of Peppy the Stunt Penguin scoffing pilchard popsicles.

Furis

Furis are the grouchiest, slouchiest hairballs in all of Monstro City. But look beyond the mops and frowns – Furis mean well, they just love getting down . . . in the dumps!

A
B
C
D
E
F
G
H
I
J
K
L
M
N
O
P
Q
R
S
T
U
V
W
X
Y
Z

Furi Fashion

This is the shop for you if your fashion tastes are stuck in the Stone Age! Furi Fashion stocks large items, many of which are related to strength, because all Furis are very large and strong (in case you hadn't noticed). Pre-historic!

Furnando - *The Mystic Moggy*

Gaze into a Mystic Moggy's eyes and you might start barking or oinking because these mysterious Moshlings are talented sorcerers. They can levitate when they meow, cough up magic furballs and make pilchards vanish (they sneak them under their top hats). Gee whiskers!

Future Falls Door

Dingle glop zip! Teleport yourself to the rest of your house through the one and only Futuristic Door.

A
B
C
D
E
F
G
H
I
J
K
L
M
N
O
P
Q
R
S
T
U
V
W
X
Y
Z

Gg

Gail

Gail Whale was among the first Monstro City residents to spot Gift Island. After achieving fame from her find, she's been watching for new discoveries and reporting via HAM Radio ever since.

A
B
C
D
E
F
G
H
I
J
K
L
M
N
O
P
Q
R
S
T
U
V
W
X
Y
Z

Gabby - *The Mini Moshifone*

Whether they're flashing up funny messages, chatting to friends, playing games or composing new ringtones, these high-tech dingalinging Moshlings are always on hand to help monsters conduct long-distance chit-chats. Just prod their fancy touchscreens and holler. It's for you hoo!

Game Starcade

Games? In your room? Youuuu betcha! Choose from Octo's Eco Adventure, Bug's Big Bounce, Sea Monster Munch and Downhill Dash. Stock up on these and invite your friends around to play.

Garlic Marshmallow

Roast'em if you dare!

The Gatekeeper

The Gatekeeper has nobody — literally, because he's just a head. But that doesn't stop him from watching over the entrance to the Super Moshis' volcanic HQ 24/7. Said to have once topped the tallest totem pole in TikkiHaahaa, this key-loving guardian is a stickler for rules: if he doesn't like the look of you, you're not getting in — it's more than his job's worth!

Giant Watch

The Giant Watch stopped working long ago, but it tells the right time twice a day! Plus, it's the object of Mini Ben's affections.

Gift Island

The one place in Moshi world where it could always be Twistmas, thanks to all the piles of presents lying around the place! It's here that Moshi Monsters can use their hard-earned Rox to buy gifts for their friends at the Gift Shop. In fact, the Gift Shop itself even looks like a present! The gifts are manufactured at the fantastic factory located on the island.

General Fuzuki
- The Warrior Wombat

Many moons ago, Warrior Wombats were used to guard intergalactic shiny stuff. But that's not because these furry little Moshlings are fearless. It's because they don't need any sleep. Or do they? New research shows that their open eyes are actually little cake tins welded to their funny hats. This allows them to take forty winks on the sly. Napping on the job? Now that's naughty!

Giant Paperclip

Rumoured to have been used by J.K. Growling to hold her *Furi Potter* manuscript together, these Giant Paperclips really go the extra mile.

Gigi - *The Magical Mule*

Magical Mules are powerful Moshlings descended from enchanted carousel horses. Maybe that's why they trot along humming fairground tunes, occasionally gliding up and down as if still attached to a merry-go-round. Totally bewitching, these elegant gee-gees love ballroom dancing and can even create rainbows. Often mistaken for Lunicorns, Magical Mules are unique as their unihorns are actually ice cream cones held on with liquorice shoelaces.

Gilbert Finnster

Gilbert Finnster's love of Moshlings began when he was just a tadpole. Monitoring his Moshling Garden daily, he began a quest to provide Moshling codes and memorabilia to his friends. When Moe Yukky suggested he might profit from his ventures, Gil saved his paper round money and opened a shop.

POSTCARD SHOP

GIFT SHOP

MONSTA-GRAMS

Gingersnap - *The Whinger Cat*

Moany, lazy but strangely charming, Whinger Cats are said to be really good at fixing things. Nobody knows if it's true because they never bother showing up. Maybe it's because they're busy waiting for other things – like bedtime and dinnertime. If you do come across one, don't expect it to move unless you've got a big handful of melted cheese because food is almost as important to these lovable layabouts as sleep. Yawn!

Gingerbread Monster

Why munch a man when you can munch a monster?

Gingerbread Wallpaper

Be careful your monster doesn't eat all the way through.

Giuseppe Gelato

Giuseppe Gelato the Ice-Scream man is so eager to serve the next customer that he often tells others to scram before they get served. Next time you're on Ooh La Lane stop by and help him keep his customers satisfied. You can even earn some Rox while you're at it!

Glooble

Gulp it down and it'll wobble all the way down your throat.

Gloop Soup

It's that Gloopy Soupy goodness that sticks to your tongue.

Glump-a-Tron 3000

A monstrous machine designed by Dr. Strangeglove which turns cute, loveable Moshlings into mean and grumpy Glumps. But then you'd be grumpy too if you'd just been Glumped!

GLUMPING SPEED!

Glump Cakes

Glumps love cakes as much as the next monster. These delicious delicacies are available in flavours like curry, cabbage and cucumber!

Glumponauts

Glumps pumped up on First Officer Ooze's goo, making them beefier and badder than ever. The technology behind Splutnik's jetpack was used to create transport for the Glumponauts.

Glumps

Glumps (scientific name *glumpitus ugllus*) are created by the criminal mastermind Dr. Strangeglove, from ordinary Moshlings, using a powerful machine of his own devising. These cheeky critters now act as his mischievous minions.

'Go Do The Hoodoo'

The track by Big Bad Bill and the Woolly Blue Hoodoos that appears on the *Music Rox* album.

Goblin Gateau

So good, you can't stop goblin it!

A B C D E F G H I J K L M N O P Q R S T U V W X Y Z

Gombala Gombala Jungle

Located on Music Island, it's in the Gombala Gombala Jungle that you'll find the Woolly Hoodoos as well as CocoLoco the Naughty Nutter.

Goober Gulch

Goober Gulch is where Nattering Nutlings can usually be found flicking through the latest Ruby Scribblez book.

Gooey Galleon

A spooky shipwreck off the coast of Music Island, home to Captain Codswallop and his ghostly crew.

Gooey Glam Rock

Gooey Glam Rock is a style of music performed by singers and musicians who wear outrageous clothes and make-up, whilst sporting outrageous hairstyles. They are particularly fond of platform-soled boots and glitter – lots of glitter! With its catchy chorus lines and thumping beats, once it's in your head it's hard to get it out again! (Rather like chewing gum in a carpet.)

The Googenheim

The Roarkers sure have designed some wacky buildings over the years, but the Googenheim Art Gallery has to be the wibbliest and wobbliest by far!

Goopy Friend

Everyone needs a Goopy Friend in their life, especially a gooperstar in the making or a goo-loving Glump. Pink, squidgy and incredibly friendly, make your new BFF a Goopy Friend.

A
B
C
D
E
F
G
H
I
J
K
L
M
N
O
P
Q
R
S
T
U
V
W
X
Y
Z

Goosebump Manor

Watch out for things that go bump in the night in this Halloween haunted house! There are Glump-o-lanterns galore for sale in Rare 'n' Scare too.

Grande Gateau

Not one, not two, but three layers of yummy gateaux. Eat in moderation.

Gracie - *The Swishy Missy*

Get your skates on! If you wanna catch a Swishy Missy you'll need to be an expert on the ice because these figure-skating Moshlings are unstoppable. When they are not twirling, jumping and performing toe-jumps on the Frostipop Glacier, Swishies are, erm, pretty clumsy. That's because they refuse to take their magic skates off, even at bedtime.

Green

There's nothing quite like a big luscious lump of Green, washed down with a hearty Cup O Gruel. It will keep you nourished for hours of arduous adventuring.

Green Slime Wallpaper

Schmooze your guests with ooze.

A
B
C
D
E
F
G
H
I
J
K
L
M
N
O
P
Q
R
S
T
U
V
W
X
Y
Z

A
B
C
D
E
F
G
H
I
J
K
L
M
N
O
P
Q
R
S
T
U
V
W
X
Y
Z

Gross-ery Store

The Gross-ery store is run by Snozzle Wobbleson. He started out as a stock monster, before being promoted to the position of cashier. He loves his job and is always concocting new and tasty treats. However, you won't find him lingering in the jelly aisle for too long!

Gumball Machine

Your very own Gumball Machine for your very own room. Get one today!

Gurgle
- The Performing Flappasaurus

Roll up, roll up! Performing Flappasauruses are the entertaining little Moshlings that always have a trick up their wings. The tricks usually go wrong, but it's best to applaud because these jolly dinos are very sensitive. If a magic routine goes really badly they've been known to burst into tears and toast their props with a burst of fiery breath. But hey, that's showbiz. Ta-daa!

Hh

Hair Clippings Rug

It's a techni-coloured dream rug, all the way from Wiggy Wonderland!

Hairy Green Paw Chair

Who knew? The lap of luxury is actually a lap ...in a Hairy Green Paw Chair!

Halloween

Spooky skies and Jack O'Lanterns, a dark and stormy Monstro City... It must be Halloween!

Handy Van Hookz

Washing the dishes in shark-infested seas is never a good idea – as Handy found out to his cost! Thankfully this merry ghost is too busy whizzing along the ship's rigging to worry about his missing mitts. Oh yes, he hates eating peas – aaarr, fiddly!

Hansel - *The Psycho Gingerboy*

Don't be fooled by the fancy frosting, plump raisins and biscuity cuteness — Psycho Gingerboys are naughty little troublemakers. When they're not stealing sweeties and holding up bakeries, they like hanging around on street corners and tripping up passers-by with their delicious but deadly candy canes. Thankfully, Psycho Gingerboys are easy to catch as they can't help dropping yummy crumbs wherever they go. You have been warned!

Hangar Eight -and-a-Half

Where is Hangar Eight-and-a-Half? No one knows except Wurley and the other Tiddlycopters who spend their days lazily hovering around this top secret location.

Happy Smiley Ovens Inc.

Happy Smiley Ovens Inc. makes food the way you like it — with a happy smile grilled in to the top.

The Hard Sock Café

One of Monstro City's top music venues, known for hosting a number of not-so-secret secret gigs.

A
B
C
D
E
F
G
H
I
J
K
L
M
N
O
P
Q
R
S
T
U
V
W
X
Y
Z

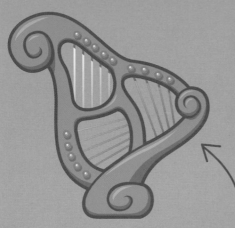

Harmony Harp

Pluck yourself a harmonic little tune. Perhaps the 'Dance of the Sugar Plum Furi'?

The Hatekeeper

Grumpy guardian of the Fiery Castle, the Hatekeeper is second cousin to the good ol' Gatekeeper of the Volcano. There's no love lost between these riddle-spewing relatives because the Hatekeeper still resents the fact that the Gatekeeper once topped the tallest totem pole in TikkiHaahaa while he was stuck at the bottom. Oh well, at least the passing Puppies loved him!

Haunted Hornament

With glowing eyes and a purple hue, the Haunted Hornament might be out to get you.

The Headmaster

Caught playing a hypnotic organ at the Super Moshiversity, he was certainly up to no good. Turned out the Headmaster was a card carrying member of C.L.O.N.C.!

A
B
C
D
E
F
G
H
I
J
K
L
M
N
O
P
Q
R
S
T
U
V
W
X
Y
Z

Heart Balloon

Let your love fly high with this hearty balloon! Tiamo would be proud.

Heart-shaped Beanbag

A lovely beanbag in the lovely shape of a lovely heart. Well, what were you expecting?

Herman Crab

Shy and retiring, except when he's with his crabby friends, Herman Crab can usually be found hanging out in the sun on Bleurgh Beach or paddling in its rock pools.

HighPants Productions

HighPants Productions is owned by Simon Growl, Talent Scout, Producer and H.A.R.G.G. – that's Handsome All Round Good Guy.

Hip Hoppity Hop Hop

Hop on one of these hip hoppity hop hops and bop till you drop!

HipHop - *The Blaring Boombox*

Say 'wassup' to Blaring Boomboxes, the playful noisemakers who just can't stop rockin' to the bang beat boogie that blares from their speakers day and night. Obsessed with old-school tunes, they love sharing their music with other Moshlings. Just make sure you don't press their 'record' button because it erases their memories. Oops!

Hipsta Hills

Favourite hangout of Flashy Foxes, like Blingo.

Hissy - *The Jazzy Wiggler*

'Psst . . .' No, it's not a secret, it's the noise Jazzy Wigglers make whenever they hear a wild tune. Distant relatives of Beatnik Boas, these way-cool Moshlings can't resist making jazzy sounds 24/7 by poking out their tongues and shaking their jellybean tail rattles. Put simply, they don't wanna hiss a thing!

Honey - *The Funny Bunny*

Dedicated followers of fashion, Funny Bunnies are the best-dressed Moshlings in town. When they're not busy texting jokes to their friends, they can be found yacking about carrot cake, clothes and fur straighteners. Talking of straightening, Funny Bunnies have one floppy ear. Experts think this is caused by listening to silly ringtones all day.

Holga - *The Happy Snappy*

Say cheese and strike a pose! Happy Snappies are the Moshlings that just love taking photos, especially if there's a famous monster in town. Get the picture? You will because they can't resist handing out snaps to everyone they meet.

Hong Bong Island

Hong Bong Island is where you'll find Bashful Bowlheads and Kittens of Good Fortune, either searching for fortune cookies in the Terry Aargh Keys or keeping themselves to themselves down in Won Ton Bay.

A
B
C
D
E
F
G
H
I
J
K
L
M
N
O
P
Q
R
S
T
U
V
W
X
Y
Z

Hoodoo Calypso

It's the hip jungle vibe that throbs through the Gombala Gombala Jungle. If limbo's your thing then you'll soon be swaying like a Moshling to the calypso's up-beat tempo. Big Bad Bill and the Woolly Blue Hoodoos love to limbo to this classic calypso rhythm, as is clear from their breakthrough hit 'Go Do the Hoodoo'.

Hoolio - *the Creepy Crooner*

Dead good on the guitar, Creepy Crooners are the wandering minstrels who love playing mournful *mariachi* music, especially when there is a full moon. With their colourful make-up and snazzy outfits they can often be found in posh Moshi restaurants serenading diners, handing out dead roses and collecting tips in their hats. How romantic!

Horrods

Run by Mizz Snoots, Horrods is the finest shop in Monstro City. Never knowingly underhowled, you won't believe their prices! It also sells some of the rarest items, such as the Platinum Pants of Power!

Hot Silly Peppers

Combine Hot Silly Peppers with Magic Beans and you might just end up attracting Sooki-Yaki. Combine Hot Silly Peppers with Love Berries and a pink Crazy Daisy and you could bag a Baby Blockhead.

A
B
C
D
E
F
G
H
I
J
K
L
M
N
O
P
Q
R
S
T
U
V
W
X
Y
Z

Hoverboard

Whatever you do, wear a helmet. These hoverboards have a mind of their own.

Hula Hoop

Don't get too dizzy! The Hula Hoop is a great way to get exercise. (Hula music not included.)

Hum Plum

Hum Plum works day in and day out, gathering invisible syrup for her children. Never a complaint leaves her lips... even when her hungry brood speak with their mouths full, causing a terrible invisible mess!

Hot Wings - *The Ragamuffin Puffin*

Easy now, Ragamuffin Puffins never get in a flap. That's not because they're super chilled out, it's because they can't fly. Not to worry though, these upbeat Moshlings are usually too busy squawking cheerful songs and performing their signature Rub-A-Dub dance moves to think about going anywhere.

A
B
C
D
E
F
G
H
I
J
K
L
M
N
O
P
Q
R
S
T
U
V
W
X
Y
Z

Humongous Haven

This larger-than-life isle makes even Elmore the Great feel small. Visit Baz Barnacle's shop to pick up some of the giant items Cap'n Buck has brought back from his travels.

Hypno-Lolly

Warning: Licking this lolly in a circle may cause the licker to quack like a duck.

Hypno-Tron

You are getting sleepy ... very, very sleepy ... when you wake up, you will buy the Hypno-Tron and click on it to hypnotize your friends ...

Humphrey
- *The Snoring Hickopotumus*

Yee-hah! Quit lollygagging around and say howdy to the Moshlings that love digging, sowing, milking and mowing. If they're not busy working the ranch, Snoring Hickos enjoy grabbing forty winks under the shade of a wacky windmill. Trouble is forty winks often turns into forty hours and that's a mighty long time when you're supposed to be mixing lazy daisy moonshine.

A
B
C
D
E
F
G
H
I
J
K
L
M
N
O
P
Q
R
S
T
U
V
W
X
Y
Z

Ii

'I Heart Moshlings'

'I Heart Moshlings' is the cutesy track by the huggalicious popstar Poppet that appears on the *Music Rox* album.

Ice-Scream

A delicious treat available at Giuseppe Gelato's Ice-Scream store on Ooh La Lane. Extra sprinkles please!

Icky

Icky the Gloop Monster is seventy-six Mr. Snoodles high and loves gloop! He has been sighted throughout history, but until now there's been no conclusive proof he exists! It is said that the Gloop Monster replenishes

I.G.G.Y. - *The Pixel-Munching Snaffler*

Aargh! Curse those pesky cursors! These pixel-scoffing Moshlings look innocent enough, but the second they spot a pointy arrow, it's history. Experts believe they find cursors really annoying – like flies flittering around their heads. Seeing as they can't swat them (they've got no arms, let alone rolled-up newspapers) they gobble them instead. 'Ulp!

I.G.G.Y. Champ Poster

I.G.G.Y. won the third annual Moshling World Cup, for the third time! His achievement was commemorated with this I.G.G.-tastic poster.

gloop supplies when he visits.

I.G.G.Y. Hat

This Pixel-Munching hat
will look fab on your monster.

Inspiration Bulb

Click it on and you might just
get a bright idea!

Iron Furnace

A fiery furnace for your monster's
house. Toasty!

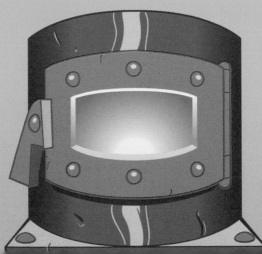

A
B
C
D
E
F
G
H
I
J
K
L
M
N
O
P
Q
R
S
T
U
V
W
X
Y
Z

J j

Jack O' Lantern

Rumour says that, once a year, these lanterns return to life and become the monsters they used to be! Spooky!

Jamtastic Crunchee

Combine with the Cookie Stacker for jam-filled tower building.

Jar of Glowbugs

Colourful little bugs to light up your room.

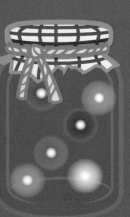

Jaunty Jack

Named after the soggy paper hat in which he keeps his fish fingers, Jaunty Jack is always happy to help Moshi landlubbers. It's just a shame that there's a price on his head (he keeps that under his hat ... alongside his pickled eggs).

A
B
C
D
E
F
G
H
I
J
K
L
M
N
O
P
Q
R
S
T
U
V
W
X
Y
Z

Jeepers Creepers Jazz

Some say that Jeepers Creepers Jazz originated in the Barmy Swarmi Jungle, others say that the musical style started in the Whoop 'n' Holler Valley. What is clear is that it's a musical style that makes good use of blue notes, improvisation, polyrhythms, syncopation and the swung note – whatever that is!

Jelly Baked Beans

Beans, beans – the magical fruit! Now in baked jelly form.

Jeepers - *The Snuggly Tiger Cub*

These adorable Moshlings really have earned their stripes. That's because they spend ages painting them on using inka-inka juice, squeezed from rare thumpkin seeds. Sadly the jungle is green, not yellow and stripy. When they're not slopping hopeless camouflage around, Snuggly Tiger Cubs love sharpening their claws and licking old swoonafish cans.

Jelly Bean Day

THE day for jelly beans! To celebrate this jelliness of a day, you must eat everything you can find with jelly beans in it, and surround yourself with all that is jelly and all that be bean.

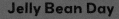

Jessie - *The Ginger McMoshling*

Thought to be distant descendants of the legendary Sock Less Monster, Ginger McMoshlings look a bit like mini Jabbersauruses – ancient creatures that roamed the world of Moshi before the Great Custard Flood. These tartan-clad critters love a wee jig whenever they hear the drone of the sagpipes. It's hilarious, especially when they pull off their false beards (which are glued to their hats) and wear 'em as kilts. Och-aye!

Jetpack

Soar to new heights with the one-of-a-kind Jetpack from Futuristic Falls.

Jokebot

Jokebot is the *Rhapsody 2's* rubbish robo-comedian. Here's one of his winners: "Where do cows go at the weekend? To the mooooovies!"

Jollywood

Mysterious and mystical, a land east of here, hot spicy flavours and hip atmosphere, with lots of colours and fierce pumping beats, where Moshi rickshaws cruise bustling streets. See steamy jungles, explore mountains high, watch mystic gurus, sit back kiss the sky, take tea on the verandah things could not be grander ... That's Jollywood!

A
B
C
D
E
F
G
H
I
J
K
L
M
N
O
P
Q
R
S
T
U
V
W
X
Y
Z

Jollywood Jive

Like a faster version of Singaling Swing, Jollywood Jive is an energetic musical and dance style popular in the lands east of Music Island. The Jollywood Jive is fast and energetic, full of fierce pumping beats – accompanied by pointy hand gestures and dancing sideways across the stage – and is becoming increasingly popular in Monstro City, thanks to the mantra-inspired warblings of Jollywood legend Bobbi SingSong.

Judder - *The Unhinged Jackhammer*

These manic Moshlings just love boinging up and down, even when there isn't a road to ruin. Used by Roarkers to smash up the streets of Monstro City and beyond, Unhinged Jackhammers should be handled with care – once they start juddering they ignore everything else around them. W-w-w-woah!

Jungle Temple Idol

Legend has it that the idol was placed here by a mysterious ancient tribe of dancing monsters! Now the Green Hoodoos worship it.

Kk

Kate Giggleton

Born in a humble Moshi area near the Icky Underpass, Kate Giggleton hit the headlines when she met Prince Sillyham. As the glamorous half of Monstro City's most famous couple, Kate enjoys counting her mountains of Rox, lunching on Ooh La Lane and giggling at her good fortune. She also loves partying with celeb friends and collecting SkyPonies. Tally ho!

Katsumas

Mess with a Katsuma and you'll unleash a flurry of claws, jaws and lightning-fast moves! When Katsumas aren't bustin' choptastic moves, they're busy working on their super-smooth style!

Katsuma Klothes

If kung-fu clothing is your thing, then you should stop by and check out Katsuma Klothes some time. The whole establishment is choptastic.

Ken Tickles

Ken Tickles isn't the happiest Roarker in Monstro City. Envious of his colleague, Bjorn Squish, he works twice as hard to be noticed, and still doesn't attract any attention. What we do notice is three eyes are better than one when precision drilling is involved.

A
B
C
D
E
F
G
H
I
J
K
L
M
N
O
P
Q
R
S
T
U
V
W
X
Y
Z

Kissy - *The Baby Ghost*

It's hard being scary when you're as cute as a Baby Ghost. These supernatural Moshlings are more interested in tutus, toys, false eyelashes and pink ribbons than sneaking around frightening Moshi Monsters. If you do see a Baby Ghost, try not to breathe near it or it might evaporate, leaving just a bow and a pair of soggy pink pumps.

Kitties

Cantankerous Whinger Cats, highly huggable Tubby Huggishis, toffee-nosed Pretty Kitties and geeky Tabby Nerdicats – you'll find them all in the Kitties Moshlings set. They're simply purrfect!

King Toot - *The Funky Pharaoh*

Sometimes mistaken for Swingin' Sphinxes, Funky Pharaohs are seriously cool Moshlings who love tootling away on their solid gold saxophones. Unfortunately they are terrible musicians. But keep that to yourself or you might get turned into a sandcastle. How? It's easy thanks to that spell-spitting cobra headband. Parp!

Kookie Cuckoo Clock

Cuckoos don't get any kookier than the one in this clock!

A
B
C
D
E
F
G
H
I
J
K
L
M
N
O
P
Q
R
S
T
U
V
W
X
Y
Z

Ll

A Lad in a Lamp

How did this lad get in this lamp? It's a mystery we may never solve. He likes it though.

Lady Meowford - *The Pretty Kitty*

Pretty Kitties are frightfully sweet, but a bit annoying. That's because these cute Moshlings are always right about everything. Well OK, there was one time when a Pretty Kitty thought it was wrong, but it turned out to be right all along. Slightly snooty, but impossibly charming, Pretty Kitties are very musical and have incredibly high-pitched singing voices. They can also speak several languages, are very good skiers, fabulous lacrosse players and know everything about everything.

Lava Lamp

Ouch! You don't want to touch this when it's hot, but it will light up your life a treat... or at least your monster's room.

A
B
C
D
E
F
G
H
I
J
K
L
M
N
O
P
Q
R
S
T
U
V
W
X
Y
Z

91

Lefty

After joining Cap'n Buck's seaworthy crew and suffering an injury in a sword fight with a seagull, Lefty found himself unable to stay balanced on deck. Buck quickly moved him to the crow's nest where he watches for new islands to visit.

Lavender Troggs

Lavender Troggs is the Moshi genius who flew through school in only two years. Despite all manner of achievements – including singing in the school choir, playing for the Moshling Chess Club and being president of Geeks and Freaks Anonymous – Lavender dabbled in his own strange science and ancient 'Walla Walla Hoohaa' magic before going on to become none other than the moustache-twirling villain Dr. Strangeglove (an anagram of Lavender Troggs!)!

Lenny Lard

Challenged by his schoolmates to become Monstro City's first youth diver, Lenny Lard has been practising in the waters of The Port ever since. Even though he can't yet swim it's said he can project himself out of the water faster than a rocket ship, but only when nobody is watching.

Leo - *The Abominable Snowling*

When they're not making ice sculptures or huge snowmen these snow-munching Moshlings love chucking snowballs, playing snow angels and decorating their igloos with chocolate sprinkles. That's because they live on a diet of snow, ice and slush, so everything they make gets eaten before it melts.

Level 50 Club

'Level 50?!?' You'd better believe it! Best practise your puzzles if you want to join the ranks of Monstro City's brightest and brainiest. Just imagine how cool you'd look with this plaque on your wall!

Liberty - *The Happy Statue*

With a lipsmackin' ice cream in one hand and a never-ending wish list in the other, Happy Statues believe in having fun, playing games and making wishes. They even wear magical crowns that glow every time they think up a new wish. It's not that these cheerful Moshlings are greedy, they just adore dreaming about yummy treats, cool clothes and twinkly trinkets. You go, girl!

Lickable Lounger

This tongue-tingling, taste bud-topped chair sure is the tops. Mmm, tasty!

Long Beard - *The Valiant Viking*

Prepare for suspect sagas of battle, bravery and broken helmet horns because Valiant Vikings are the ocean-going Moshlings who can't stop babbling on about their dubious exploits. When they are not pillaging pickled goods, these beardy old fogies love play-acting with their rubber hammers.

Lila Tweet

Lila Tweet spends her time picnicking with her friend Pete Slurp and checking her room for five star ratings. She's the best singer in her school and her mum makes the best Quenut Butter Sandwiches in Monstro City.

Lock Clock

The Lock Clock is so awesome you'll want to keep it under lock and key.

Loopy Liquid

A funky decoration for any home, this laboratory equipment that would be just the thing for Tamara Tesla.

The Lost Treasure of Umba Umba

A stupendous stash of ultra-powerful Rox. But where's it hidden? Well, if we knew that it wouldn't be lost, would it?

Love Berries

If you want to attract Pilfering Toucans, Batty Bubblefish or Whinger Cats, then these are the seeds you'll need.

Luckies

Ladybirds, horseshoes, four-leaf clover, wishing wells, falling stars, wishbones, the number seven – they're all supposed to be lucky. However, none of them are as lucky as the person who manages to attract one to their Moshling garden!

Luvlis

Luvlis are flutterly amazing with a sprinkling of magical hokery-pokery! You never know if they'll wow you with their star-tipped stems. It's enough to give you glittery goosebumps!

Luvli Looks

Luvli Looks is a clothes shop that sells everything from feather boas and beauty spots, to earrings and necklaces. They even do a line in roses! The feminine clothes on sale mainly fit Luvlis, but some can be re-sized to fit Poppets.

Lurgee- *the Sniffly Splurgee*

Please wash your hands, Sniffly Splurgees are highly infectious – in a good way, because despite the constant coughs and sniffles these friendly, bacteria-loving Moshlings soak up germs and viruses, keeping the world of Moshi bug-free. In fact the only downside to owning a Sniffly Splurgee is that they stink of cough syrup. Yuck!

Lush Lagoon

Pilfering Toucans nest high in the palm trees near Lush Lagoon.

Mm

Magic Beans

These beans really are bona fide Magic Beans. How else is it that they can attract the likes of Angel the SkyPony and Pooky the Potty Pipsqueak to your Moshling Garden?

Magic Mirror

This is one of the rarest items in Monstro City. If you find one, look deep and see if you can unlock its mystical powers.

Main Street

This is the busiest bustlingest place in Monstro City. It's here you'll find Snozzle Wobbleson's Gross-ery Store, Yukea (which is owned by Moe Yukky), Bizarre Bazaar, the Moshling Seed Cart, the EN-GEN power plant and the headquarters of *The Daily Growl*.

A
B
C
D
E
F
G
H
I
J
K
L
M
N
O
P
Q
R
S
T
U
V
W
X
Y
Z

WELCOME TO MONSTRO CITY

GROSS-ERY STORE

MOSHLING SEEDS

OPEN

YUKEA

BIZARRE BAZAAR

EN-GEN

The Daily Growl

NO NEWS IS GOOD NEWS.

Make-Believe Valley

Home to Potty Pipsqueaks and cardboard box spaceships.

Marshmallow Pillow

A pillow made of a marshmallow. What will those crazy cats come up with next?

Mavis the Figurehead

As the enchanted figurehead of the *Gooey Galleon*, Mavis can remember the days before the crew became ghostified. Don't bother asking her about it – she's usually too busy humming spooky songs and bobbing for pilchards.

Max Volume

Max Volume can shake the room with his mega-amped boom box, but unfortunately he can't move from his current position. With noise ordinances in front of local shops, and a broken volume control panel, Max is trapped until his boom box batteries are drained.

A B C D E F G H I J K L M N O P Q R S T U V W X Y Z

McNulty - *The Undercover YapYap*

Psst . . . guess what? Undercover YapYaps are the nosy puppies that love sniffing out secrets, rummaging through drawers and going "psst". With their plain fur and cuddlesome looks these cute little snoops can dupe their way into any situation, but they are also masters of disguise. In fact the only way to be sure you're dealing with one is to look out for that incredibly waggy tail. It's a dead giveaway!

McScruff

The naughtiest, saltiest scallywag ever to walk the plank, McScruff is forever playing practical jokes on his shipmates. Luckily he scares easy and can't swim without armbands. He also plays a mean squeezebox!

Meringue Meadow

Dinky Dreamclouds are native to Meringue Meadow, an area surrounded by towering vanilla pod trees and wild candyfloss.

A
B
C
D
E
F
G
H
I
J
K
L
M
N
O
P
Q
R
S
T
U
V
W
X
Y
Z

Micro Dave - *The Popty-Ping*

What's cookin'? Why it's a Popty-Ping! Often mistaken for Grinning Goggleboxes, these jolly Moshlings are the hottest critters in town. Ask one to heat up some gloop soup or defrost your Mutant Sprouts and it will be glad to oblige. It might even give you a high five – but take care because those oven mitts get really hot. Ping!

Mermaiden's Seahair

What Mermaiden is complete without her flowing locks of seaweed?

Mice Krispies

Burrow into these delicious treats before they snap, crackle, and pop away!

Mini Ben - *The Teeny TickTock*

'CLONG!' Don't be alarmed – Teeny TickTocks are the noisy Moshlings that love chiming on the hour, every hour. When they're not swaying to and fro, making their bells go bong, these terribly old-fashioned chaps enjoy waxing their bushy moustaches, nibbling cucumber sandwiches and asking everyone the time. Have you ever tried looking at a clock that's stuck on top of your head? It's harder than you think!

Mississippi Mud Pie

Now with real mud! Yum!

Missy Kix

Missy Kix is the sassy secret agent/musician from far-off Moshimo City. Already a mega-gooperstar over there, she's since taken the rest of the Moshi World by storm. It's all down to a combination of her hyper catchy dance tracks, super cool fashion sense and a variety of super-secret agent skills.

'The Missy Kix Dance'

Missy Kix's Moshimo City Pop dance track appears on *Music Rox*, the first Moshi Monsters album.

A
B
C
D
E
F
G
H
I
J
K
L
M
N
O
P
Q
R
S
T
U
V
W
X
Y
Z

Mizz Snoots

Winning several beauty pageants and a scholarship to OxSnout University, Mizz Snoots has always held her head high. When she's not busy selling extravagant items at Horrods, she can be seen in the pages of *Miss Preen Magazine*.

Misty - *The Playful Pfft Pfft*

Spraying pretty patterns sounds like a pleasant enough hobby, but Playful Pfft Pffts can't help puffing paint over everything in sight. After all, why say it if you can spray it? Thankfully, hip gooperstars such as Blingo are starting to use these canny characters to decorate their cribs with funky artwork. (Always shake before use.)

Moe Yukky

With a name like Moe Yukky, it's surprising that he's the cleanest monster in Monstro City. He's the reigning champion of the annual Slop Moppin' Competition and he has the Golden Mop trophies to prove it. Moe keeps his shop, Yukea, pristine clean, so wipe your feet before you enter!

Monsieur Macabre's Mansion

This spooky little mansion holds the tiniest, growliest monsters of all.

Monster Plant

Keep your eye on this cactus – it just might get away!

Monster Trucks

You ain't never seen a truck ROAR like these ones!

A
B
C
D
E
F
G
H
I
J
K
L
M
N
O
P
Q
R
S
T
U
V
W
X
Y
Z

WELCOME TO MONSTRO CITY!

A B C D E F G H I J K L M N O P Q R S T U V W X Y Z

Monstro City

Whether you're just passing through or staying for a long time, from Sludge Street to Ooh La Lane, Monstro City has everything any discerning monster needs. If shopping's your thing there are clothes shops galore and the Yukea furniture store as well. Looking for a bit of culture? Why not check out the Googenheim Art Gallery? If you're feeling peckish pop along to Snozzle Wobbleson's Gross-ery Store on Main Street, or the Ice-Scream Shop on Ooh La Lane.

Monstro City Marketplace

The Monstro City Marketplace is the shopping centre for clothes. The shops you'll find here are Diavlo's Duds, Furi Fashion, Katsuma Klothes, Luvli Looks, Poppet's Closet and Zommer's Drop Dead Threads. So what are you waiting for? Check you've got your Rox and get shopping!

MARKETPLACE Monstro City NOW OPEN!

EXIT POPPET'S CLOSET ZOMMER'S DROP DEAD THREADS LUVLI LOOKS FURI FASHION DIAVLO'S DUDS KATSUMA KLOTHES

Moon Orchid

Very attractive to werewolves . . . luckily there aren't any in Monstro City! Pretty Kitties, Princess Ponies and Rummaging Plotamuses all love Moon Orchids.

Mooshroom

It's purple and it's sticky, and not altogether icky.

'Moptop TweenyBop (My Hair's Too Long)'

Zack Binspin's breakthrough hit single, featuring a rap by the flashiest Flashy Fox, Blingo.

Moshi Cupcakes

Help Hansel the Gingerboy and create your very own cupcakes to attract hungry Moshlings.

The Moshi MonStars

The Moshi MonStars are the *real* stars of the *Music Rox* album. The six monsters that make up the band auditioned at the Underground Disco in front of Simon Growl, Tyra Fangs and Simon's Wiggy Thingy, as part of HighPants Productions' Monstro City's Got The Ex-Idol Pop Factor competition. The group's biggest hit to date is 'The Moshi Monsters Theme.'

'The Moshi Monsters Theme'

The Moshi MonStars' track on the *Musix Rox* album.

Moshi Fun Park

This is where the Moshis like to hang out and challenge each other to a whole range of cool games.

Moshi Happy Snaps

You'll need a keen eye and fast reflexes to play this Moshi mini-game. Grab your camera, and get clicking!

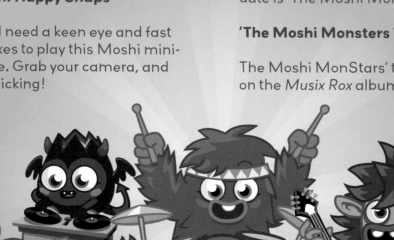

Moshi Monsters Trophies

Everyone can be a winner with these roarsome level-up trophies!

Moshi Star Signs

The star signs of the Moshi Horrorscope range from A-squirt-ius through Snoore-us and Leo-bot to Capri-cauldron.

'Moshi Twistmas'

The festive track that tops the charts every Twistmas in Moshi world.

Moshimo City Pop

Electronic dance music that's hit the big time in far-off Moshimo City, Moshimo City Pop might have its origins in rock but is now purely pop. Featuring lots of keyboards, samplers, techno drumbeats and other digital sound effects, Missy Kix's breakthrough track 'The Missy Kix Dance' is pure Moshimo City Pop.

A
B
C
D
E
F
G
H
I
J
K
L
M
N
O
P
Q
R
S
T
U
V
W
X
Y
Z

A
B
C
D
E
F
G
H
I
J
K
L
M
N
O
P
Q
R
S
T
U
V
W
X
Y
Z

Moshlings

Moshlings are cute, cool and collectible creatures for your Moshi Monsters to collect.

HOT SILLY PEPPERS

MOON ORCHID

STAR BLOSSOM

SNAP APPLE

DRAGON FRUIT

LOVE BERRIES

MAGIC BEANS

CRAZY DAISY

Moshling Seeds

Available in Star Blossom, Love Berries, Dragon Fruit, Crazy Daisy, Magic Beans, Snap Apple, Moon Orchid and Hot Silly Peppers.

Moshling Boshling

Fire friendly Moshlings from a giant catapult to take out those conniving, cake-swiping Glumps.

Moshling Garden

Moshi Monster, quite contrary, how does your Moshling Garden grow? All that depends on what combination of seeds you plant. You never know, you might even catch that elusive ultra-rare Moshling you've been after for so long. And keep an eye out for Rox flowers!

Moshling Zoo

So once you've collected a whole gaggle of Moshlings what are you going to do with them ... other than put them in your very own Moshling Zoo to keep them safe and well?

Mount CharChar

On the Isle of Emberooze you'll find gasoline-glugging Fiery Frazzledragons soaring in the thermals over Mount CharChar.

Mr. Meowford

Mr. Meowford is actually the Lord of Catberley Manor, working undercover as a fisherman, even though he and Lady Meowford are made of money. It started as a school project about the working cat, and became Lord Meowford's favourite pastime.

Mr. Snoodle - *The Silly Snuffler*

Silly Snufflers are some of the sleepiest, snuffliest Moshlings around. Whenever they amble by, monsters can't help but yawn and fall asleep on the spot, and that's how Silly Snufflers manage to avoid being caught! By the time a monster has woken up, the Snufflers have managed to (slowly) get away. Foiled again – YAWN!

Mr. Mushy Peas

Nobody knows why this peg-leg pirate wears 3-D glasses – he claims he found them under a pile of DVDs in the legendary Timeshift Trench. Or maybe he just pinched them from the souvenir shop on Hong Bong Island?

Mr. Tea

I pity the coffee-drinking fool!

Music Rox

The first Moshi Monsters album, put out by Simon Growl's HighPants Productions.

Munchies

Feeling a bit peckish? Fancy a midnight snack, or elevenses, or maybe even twelveses? A swig of Lipsmacking Bubbly or a cheeky bowl of Bashful Bowlhead could be just the thing for you.

Music Island

According to Simon Growl, Music Island is where the magic happens. Anybody who's anybody hangs out here, and you can't consider yourself a proper gooperstar until you're hanging around the Sandy Drain Hotel with Simon and his celebrity pals. The Gombala Gombala Jungle is also found on Music Island.

Mustachio

Is that facial fuzz for real or is it just a terrible disguise? Who knows, Mustachio is too busy barking orders and attacking Moshlings with scritchy-scratchy Bristly Brush Offs to answer silly questions.

A B C D E F G H I J K L M N O P Q R S T U V W X Y Z

Mutant Glump Sharks

These mutant hybrids are fiercely protective, but not very smart! Look out for them on C.L.O.N.C.'s spacestation.

Mutant Sprouts

You know how sprouts taste disgusting? Well the Mutant Sprouts of Brashcan Alley are downright dangerous! They roam the neighbourhood in packs and as much as you don't like eating sprouts, they'd have no qualms about eating you! (Available in ninja and non-ninja varieties.)

My Little Mutant

A speedy little pony if ever there was one, those six legs certainly come in handy.

Myrtle

Myrtle the Diving Turtle is world-renowned for her treasure hunting ability. Her great finds have included one teapot, a shoelace, and a pool table on which she plays weekly snooker matches with her mates.

112

Mystery Box

Buy one of these from Paws 'n' Claws then unwrap to reveal a mystery Moshling code!

Mystery Eggs

Collect the Mystery Eggs from Horrods and you'll be in for a surprise!

Mystic Orb

A floating mystical orb. But what's weirder, the orb or the hand holding it?

Mystic Wand

Wand of mystery, make me some Pop Rox – or some Slop – or just continue looking pretty.

Mythies

Their names are spoken of in hushed whispers and some barely believe that these legendary Moshlings even exist. But they do, and any avid Moshling collector can find one – if they look hard enough!

A
B
C
D
E
F
G
H
I
J
K
L
M
N
O
P
Q
R
S
T
U
V
W
X
Y
Z

Ned

Say hello to the Glump that looks like a complete nerd, but keep it quiet because behind those daft goggles Ned is a total fiend, especially when mangling Moshlings with Goggle-Plop Grapples.

New Houses Shop

Change your monster's house style and floors at the New Houses shop on Ooh La Lane.

Ninjas

Ancient legend tells how somewhere, over the rainbow, in the Land of the Surprising Sun, Ninja Moshlings once lived together in peace. Caped Assassins would train alongside Cheeky Chimps, while Warrior Wombats and Slapstick Tortoises chopped planks of wood in half – with their heads! Today, the only things they have in common are a love of sushi, kung-fu movies and the ability to speak Moshlingese.

Nipper - *The Titchy TrundleBot*

Need a hand? Better call a Titchy TrundleBot! As well as helping to build Monstro City, these versatile Moshlings can pluck Rox from the highest trees, trundle across bumpy surfaces and warn monsters of falling boulders. It's easy thanks to their stretchy flexi-arms, caterpillar-clad tootsies and flashing hats.

Nutties

The Moshlings in the Nutties set all have one thing in common – they're as sweet as a nut!

Noisies

There's a Moshling set that's making a big noise in Moshi World. So find your earplugs or stick your fingers in your lugholes, because – that's right, you guessed it – they're the Noisies!

Oo

The Observatory

Just past The Port on a rocky outcrop sits the Moshi Observatory. Tamara Tesla invents puzzles as well as other useful inventions in her lab here. If you happen to drop by, make sure you have a look through the Moshiscope then try to spot the Snoodle constellation.

Octo

Octo, the H_2O Queen, is living large in The Port. She's the spouter and spritzer of fine, fresh mist and our eco-conscious water recycler. On a nice day, she'll give you a spray that beats even the best bath.

Octo's Eco Adventure

Keep Monstro City clean! Shoot the trash before it gets in the water and score big! Buy your own arcade game at the Games Starcade.

Octopeg

Biting your
nails is daft,
but chewing
your tentacles
is plain silly.
That's why Octopeg is stumped –
literally! Being a nervous type, this
flabby fella spends most of his time
scoffing barnacles beneath the
Gooey Galleon. Yuck!

Oddie's Doughnut Dash

Help Oddie munch as much fruit as
he can without getting stuck in sticky
Ice-Scream. Play it at the Fun Park!

Oiler

Searching for underground oil
pockets is tough work, but Oiler is
happy to do the job. Keeping the
gears on Gift Island well-oiled is an
important task for this Monstro City
sea critter.

Oddie - *The Sweet Ringy Thingy*

With their doughy bodies and gloopy
icing, Sweet Ringy Thingies look
exceedingly delicious. And they are!
That's why these squishy hoops
are always on the move – everyone
wants a piece! It's a good thing they
can blast attackers with volleys of
hundreds and thousands, otherwise
they'd be extinct. If you're wondering
how a bunch of sticky doughnutters
ever became living, breathing
Moshlings, don't. It will only make
your brain ache.

A
B
C
D
E
F
G
H
I
J
K
L
M
N
O
P
Q
R
S
T
U
V
W
X
Y
Z

Ooh La Lane

This is where you'll find some of the most chic boutiques in Monstro City. Fancy cooling down with a chocolate crunch or jellyfish ice-scream? Then the Ice-Scream Shop is the place for you! And while you're there, why not check out the Googenheim Art Gallery, the Print Workshop, the Moshi Store or take the weight off your paws at Tyra's Spa?

Oompah - *The Brassy BlowyThing*

Do you like parping? Good, because these melodious Moshlings can't stop tooting thigh-slapping tunes whenever they smell sausages grilling or hear wobble-ade fizzing. Brassy BlowyThings also enjoy burping rainbow-coloured bubbles as they march along to their toot-tastic ditties. Parp!

Old Knackersville

Princess Ponies come from a humble area known as Old Knackersville near Gluey Gulch.

A
B
C
D
E
F
G
H
I
J
K
L
M
N
O
P
Q
R
S
T
U
V
W
X
Y
Z

Orchid in Bloom

Freshly plucked from the Fangdoodle Fields, this orchid never wilts.

O'Really - *The Unlucky Larrikin*

If you're looking for a stroke of luck then best look away, because Unlucky Larrikins are the most unfortunate Moshlings of all. Not that they realise it because these upbeat critters are always looking on the bright side, whistling, joking, and telling tall stories to anyone who'll listen. It must be the way they tell 'em. Zzzzzz . . .

A
B
C
D
E
F
G
H
I
J
K
L
M
N
O
P
Q
R
S
T
U
V
W
X
Y
Z

A
B
C
D
E
F
G
H
I
J
K
L
M
N
O
P
Q
R
S
T
U
V
W
X
Y
Z

Patch

Patch the seagull monitors The Port for unsavoury characters and scraps of leftovers from the fishermen. He has no problem with his left eye and only wears the eyepatch to keep up with the latest trends in *Pirate Style Magazine*.

Paws 'n' Claws

Paws 'n' Claws is owned by Gilbert Finnster. He made it his mission to provide Moshling memorabilia to other collectors.

EXIT

PAWS'N'CLAWS

OLORAMA

Log in to **MOSHIMONSTERS.COM**, click the **ENTER SECRET CODE** button and type the **FIRST WORD** on the **FIFTH LINE** used to describe **UNCLE SCALLOPS** in this book. Your surprise free gift will appear in your treasure chest!

Peacock Chair

Sit with some major fanfare in the Peacock Chair!

Peekaboo
- The Oakey-Dokey Hokey-Pokey

Is it a walking tree stump or a shy woodland critter in disguise? Who knows, because Oakey-Dokey Hokey-Pokies scurry away whenever you get near them. One thing's for sure, these highly-strung Moshlings will squirt slippy sap at anyone who tickles so much as a twig, so leaf 'em alone!

Penny - *The Mini Money*

Heads or tails? You choose because these lucky Moshlings love flipping themselves high up in the air, especially when they need to make important decisions. Rub one on its tummy and it might just bring you good luck. Ker-ching!

Peppy - *The Stunt Penguin*

Despite being rubbish at riding bikes (their feet don't reach the pedals), these cool little Moshlings are obsessed by anything with two-wheels. That's why they slide along on their tummies making vroom-vroom noises and revving the air with their stumpy wings. As well as their need for speed, Stunt Penguins scoff over a hundred pilchard popsicles a day, which they keep under their crash helmets. Yuckity yuck!

Pepper Popcorn

Sneeze through the latest blockbuster with this spicy snack available at the Gross-ery Store.

Peppergroany Rug

Groans every time you step on it!

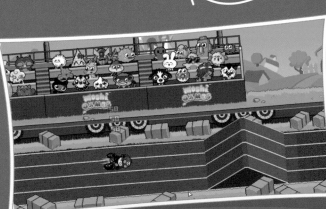

Peppy's Stuntbike

To score maximum points in this Moshi game, add stunts to your flips and pop a wheelie when you're on a straight. Pick up the arcade game at the Games Starcade.

Percy

Percy once challenged a pirate to a duel, chickened out and vowed never to sail the high seas again. A self-confessed landlubber, Percy doesn't miss the ocean at all and happily hops from roof to roof for entertainment.

Pet Seahorse

Fish shmish, what you want is a seahorse for your monster's room!

Petal Pals

Pick up a patch of Petal Pals! (There are five to collect.)

Pete Slurp

Looking for an adventurous friend? Look no further than Pete Slurp. A collector of rare slugs, Pete has built his own playhouse in his yard, and is never seen without his best mate, Lila Tweet. Pete is tone deaf, but supportive of Lila's singing career.

A
B
C
D
E
F
G
H
I
J
K
L
M
N
O
P
Q
R
S
T
U
V
W
X
Y
Z

Pirate Pong

Poo, what's that smell? Oh, it's Pirate Pong, the stinkiest Glump in town. Capable of clearing a room in seconds with a Stinky Winky Squint, this pongy pirate reeks of rotten fish and hot trash, so keep your distance.

Plank

It's a plank. Sorry, there's not a lot more to say. You wooden want me to leave now, wood you?

Pip - *The Savvy Sapling*

Savvy by name, savvy by nature these titchy woodland Moshlings know everything there is to know about nature. When they are not studying soil samples, leaping into piles of leaves and collecting berries in their little acorn hats, Savvy Saplings enjoy writing notes using enchanted sap and playing golf with twiggy clubs and mini gooberry balls.

A
B
C
D
E
F
G
H
I
J
K
L
M
N
O
P
Q
R
S
T
U
V
W
X
Y
Z

Platinum Pants of Power

Possessing Platinum Pants Proves Power. Purchase Promptly!

Pocito - *The Mini Mangler*

Tremendously strong and super-elasticky, Mini Manglers are the mysterious masked Moshlings who can't stop wrestling. If you find one practising the latest eye-watering moves do not disturb or you might find yourself in a spinning headlock with a full-nelson fajita in your face. Yuck!

Plinky - *The Squeezy TinkleHuff*

Accordion to experts, these squeezy-wheezy musical Moshlings like nothing more than having their keys tickled as they boing up and down, puffing out merry tunes and waltzing around town. But don't push their buttons – it makes 'em hiccup out of tune!

Podge

Quick, run! Podge is boinging along Main Street – and that means you might get caught in a Lumpy Lasso! It's true because Podge has a super long icky-sticky tongue – ideal for rounding up poor little Moshlings!

Pogo-Go-Go!

This is no normal pogo stick – it has the power to bounce you through the roof!

Ponies

Yee-haa! It's those thoroughbred Moshlings the Ponies! They're all here – those sleepy slow-pokes the Silly Snufflers, the celestial and secretive SkyPonies, the unihorned Magical Mules and the precocious Princess Ponies. So get your nose out of that feed bag and saddle up!

Ponies Stellar Stable

Hay! Proudly display your very own Ponies Stellar Stable replica in your room for all your NEIGH-bours to enjoy.

Pooky - *The Potty Pipsqueak*

With their cracked eggshell helmets, Playful Potty Pipsqueaks are often mistaken for newly-hatched Moshlings. They claim they wear this strange headgear to protect themselves from Killer Canaries. But why would Killer Canaries want to attack? Simple, the eggshells belong to them! Potty Pipsqueaks steal them so that they can pretend to be racing drivers and spacemen.

Poppets

Poppets are bashful, huggalicious little critters, but when no one's around, they just love to get down! It's what their titchy paws and boots were made for!

Pop Rox

Pop them in your mouth and Rox your taste buds!

A
B
C
D
E
F
G
H
I
J
K
L
M
N
O
P
Q
R
S
T
U
V
W
X
Y
Z

Poppet's Closet

Found in the Monstro City Marketplace, Poppet's Closet is a shop that specialises in outfits for Poppets! You'll find everything from Witches and Fairy costumes, through to Warrior outfits, most of which will fit any monster (if suitably re-sized).

The Port

It's yo-ho-ho and off to The Port with Captain Buck E. Barnacle, Roland Jones, Babs and more. As well as shopping for something a little special or out of the ordinary, it's from here that you can take a boat to Gift Island. Just remember to give the Rox trees a shake before embarking.

Potion Ocean

The Potion Ocean is home to all manner of Fishies and is also where you will find the new Sea Mall, where Valley Mermaids like to flounce around.

A B C D E F G H I J K L M N O P Q R S T U V W X Y Z

Pranksgiving

Start April off jumping for joy, with the hilarious arrival of Pranksgiving, when monsters are allowed to play pranks on their pals. But you'd better be prepared for some side-splitting silliness!

I GOT PRANKED!

Prince Sillyham

Genuine Moshi royalty, Prince Sillyham is the upper crust character who spends his days sipping Wobble-ade, adjusting his crown and shaking hands with his devoted fans. When he's not getting his pillows plumped by minions, the Prince enjoys throwing royal memorabilia from his Rox-plated carriage as he rides through Monstro City with Kate Giggleton. It's a tough job but someone's gotta do it!

Prickles - *The Tickly Pickle*

Yikes! It's Tickly Pickle time! As well as being incredibly prickly these potbound Moshlings are really, really tickly. Worse still, every time they sneeze they fire clouds of itching powder all over the place. And every time they scratch themselves they sneeze. Talk about irritating!

A
B
C
D
E
F
G
H
I
J
K
L
M
N
O
P
Q
R
S
T
U
V
W
X
Y
Z

Princess Poppet Music Box

The prettiest princess in town gets her own little music box. Wind it up!

Print Workshop

The Print Workshop is a store on Ooh La Lane where you can print trading cards, posters, masks and a 'how to draw a monster' booklet – all for free!

Priscilla - *The Princess Pony*

Rumoured to be descended from royalty, Princess Ponies are always fiddling with their tiaras, waving their hooves at passers-by and performing pirouettes – well anything to cause a stir. If their regal routines fail to impress, prepare to be astounded because they can make their manes and tails change colour by jingling their jewellery. One trick ponies? No way!

Prof. Purplex - *The Owl of Wiseness*

Banned by every library and bookstore in the land, Owls of Wiseness are brainier than big brain pies with extra brain sprinkles. Able to digest an entire encyclopedia in ten seconds, these birdy boffins have a real appetite for knowledge – literally, because they will scoff any book they see. If you spot one, hide your comics – pictures are worth a thousand words. Urp!

Pumpkin Chowder

Best served on Halloween, preferably in a bowl.

Prom Tuxedo

Get a bit of class – a first for Zommers – with this swish tux.

Puppies

Puppy Moshlings might look like adorable, wet-nosed, happy, yappy, tail-waggy diddy dogs, but the truth is they're totally barking! Nonetheless, these mini-mutts make great pets. Just make sure you keep them away from your Kitties, or fur will fly!

Puppies Ruff Ruff Ranch

Welcome to the doghouse! Chewed up slippers not included.

Purdy - *The Tubby Huggishi*

Tubby Huggishis are highly huggable Moshlings that spend most days preening themselves and lounging about eating piles of pastry. That's why most of them are a little on the large side. When they're not scoffing cakes, these shaggy felines enjoy giving advice to other Moshlings, dipping their paws in syrup and meow-ing to their friends about the price of lard.

Purr-Fection

Left behind in some luggage at Hictoria Station, Purr-Fection was found by frolicking school children passing by while journeying to the Moshi Fun Park. After several scary raaarghllercoaster rides, Purr was treated to a life of luxury in the school gardens.

Puzzle Palace

The Puzzle Palace is the place where you can play games and crack quizzes to earn yourself extra Rox. Play the Daily Challenge or tackle the Tricky Trivia tasks, you can even test your knowledge of Moshi Monsters with Master of Moshi!

Qq

Quick! Sand!

Build sensational sandcastles in this Moshi game. It's a beach-full of fun!

Quivering Quarry

Titchy TrundleBots are most at home playing tag in Quivering Quarry.

Queen's Throne

Feeling regal? Check out this royal treat for a seat, the Queen's Throne!

Quenut Butter Sandwich

Made with real quenuts, for the extra nutty crunch.

Rr

Raarghly

Raarghly is a monster from another world. Which world? Nobody knows. Able to play six video games at once all while watching over the Games Starcade, this monster can't be beaten! He'll be your best friend if you feed him any kind of space food. Dehydrated ice cream is his favourite.

Rainbow Shades

Ooo, rainbow shades. It's time to make everything look technicolour funtastic.

Rat Tail Spaghetti

Guaranteed free from mouse tail.

Rare & Scare

Take a walk over to Goosebump Manor and check out the all new shop, Rare & Scare. Manning, err ... ghosting the shop is Zoinks who has all kinds of cool Halloween stuff, including a few ULTRA RARE items.

Recycle Bin

'Feed me!' That's all you'll ever hear from this trash can, he's *constantly* hungry.

Reggae Reef

Reggae Reef is where you'll find Songful SeaHorses bobbing around in the shallow waters.

Rhapsody 2

This cool, hi-tech UFO crash-landed on Music Island after a close encounter of the sun-smashing kind. Inside were Captain Squirk and his Zoshling crew. The *Rhapsody 2* lay wrecked in a clearing in the revered Unknown Zone until the Super Moshis were able to help fix it.

A
B
C
D
E
F
G
H
I
J
K
L
M
N
O
P
Q
R
S
T
U
V
W
X
Y
Z

Rickety Boo

Stop! In the name of Rickety Boo! This busy-body Roarker is always pestering passers-by with his road sign, but some say he was fired ages ago and doesn't have anything better to do. Weirder still, he keeps half-eaten sandwiches under his hardhat. Well, it beats stacking cones!

Rising Sun Headband

Release the ninja kitty within with this natty headband.

Ritzy Resort

Lights, camera, action! The Secrets lounge luxuriously in this lavish living space, away from the flashbulbs of the pesky paparazzi.

Roarberry Cheesecake

What can we say about this monstrous cooked creation? Well it's louder than your average dessert.

Roaring Fireplace

Let the flames fly. Burn Burn Burrrrn!

Roary Scrawl

Roary Scrawl tirelessly types away at *The Daily Growl* office, determined to keep Monstro City informed with all the ooze that's fit to print. With all those eyes, it's only natural that he's the editor-in-chief. He spends his free time searching for his misplaced eyeballs and snoop . . . err, monster watching.

Roast Beast

Just like mother used to roast.

A
B
C
D
E
F
G
H
I
J
K
L
M
N
O
P
Q
R
S
T
U
V
W
X
Y
Z

Robot Butler

Finally! There's no better way to watch Eye TV than with your very own Robot Butler to wait on you paw and foot.

'Rock Like A Zommer'

Zommer's classic, and totally rad, Drool Metal track that he laid down for the *Music Rox* album.

Rockin' Rocking Chair

This chair was previously owned by the Monstar of Rock 'n' Roll, Pelvis Grisly.

Rock Clock

A clock that rocks on ... at least until the batteries run out.

A B C D E F G H I J K L M N O P Q R S T U V W X Y Z

Rocko

Don't you just hate Glumps? Rocko does! Then again Rocko hates everything. That's why you'll often see this snaggle-toothed brute boinging along alone before attacking with a Rocko Blocko Backroll.

Rocky - *The Baby Blockhead*

They might be stoney-faced and a little dense, but Burly Blockheads can be really helpful. That's because these super heavyweight Moshlings are very, very strong – hardly surprising as they're made from solid rock! They've even been known to sweat liquid concrete when lifting heavy objects. The trouble is they don't know their own strength and often get into trouble breaking things – especially fingers when they're shaking hands. Crr-unch!

Rofl - *The Jabbering Jibberling*

Wind 'em up and watch 'em go? Absolutely, but there's more to these mouthy Moshlings than big smiles and chattering teeth because they are completely hyperactive. As soon as they get wound up they can't stop spouting total gibberish at breakneck speed. Dousing them in chilled Gloop Soup helps stem the non-stop nonsense. Failing that, use toffee – in your ears!

A
B
C
D
E
F
G
H
I
J
K
L
M
N
O
P
Q
R
S
T
U
V
W
X
Y
Z

Rooby - *The Plucky PunchaRoo*

Say g'day and duck out of the way because Plucky PunchaRoos are the paw-swinging Moshlings that will do almost anything to protect the titchy purple critters that live in their pouches. And that's strange because the purple critters are actually soft toys stuffed with jellybeans. Crikey!

Roland Jones

Roland Jones is obsessed with Wobble-ade. Convinced it will cause growth spurts and jealous of his siblings who are more than twice his size, he buys a new bottle of Wobble-ade every fifteen minutes. With all that sloshy pop in his belly, he's often seen (and heard) rolling home.

Rox

Rox is the currency of Monstro City. You earn these colourful gems by playing games and solving puzzles located around the city. And you can also collect Rox by shaking Rox Trees at The Port.

A B C D E F G H I J K L M N O P Q R S T U V W X Y Z

Rox Flowers

Rox flowers start out as regular seeds but a rare and undefined mutation causes the flowers to bloom Rox. Instant cash-back! Ker-ching!

RoxStars

These fortunate Moshlings have forged a career in the Music Biz, including Zack Binspin, Bobbi Singsong, Hoolio the Creepy Crooner and Ziggy the Quirky Koala. Look out for their chart-toppers on the *Music Rox* album.

Roxy - *The Precious Prism*

Deep beneath the Twinkly-Dink mines lies a rich seam of Rox. But Precious Prisms don't hang out there. It's too obvious! These secret Moshlings are so precious they're scared to lay a finger on anything (including themselves!) in case they leave smudges, hence the silly white gloves. Crazier still, they often shatter into squillions of pieces. Handle with care!

Roy G. Biv

A professional Rainbow Rider, an expert Sky Surfer, and a Colossal Cloud Cruiser, Roy G. Biv is a totally rad and colourful dude. He only comes to Monstro City once a year on Roy G. Biv Day to make sure there are rainbows all year round (without the rain . . . it's MAGIC!). Watch out for his Funky Fuchsia Fakie!

Rubber Duck

Quack! Let it swim across your floor all day long.

Ruby Scribblez

Roving reporter for *Shrillboard Magazine*, top-rated talk show host, author of various Monstrous Biographies and friend to the stars, Ruby Scribblez started out writing boring labels at Yukea. Friendly but pushy, she went on to make coffee for Roary Scrawl. She's even rumoured to have dated Hairosniff's singer, Screech McPiehole.

Ss

Saffron Cake

Glump Cakes aren't just for Glumps. Save up enough Rox and reach a high enough level and a tasty Saffron Cake could be yours. Glumpalicious!

Sailor Hat

Ahoy there, sailor! This seaworthy headgear will make even the fishiest of Fishies feel right at home.

The Sandy Drain Hotel

Where do the cooooolest Moshi megastars hang out when not on tour? Why the Sandy Drain Hotel, of course! With its spa huts and gourmet restaurant, guitar-shaped pool and cooling cascade, what better way could there be to chill-ax than in this heavenly haven? Besides, it only costs five million Rox a night to stay there!

A Sauce of Course

Improves any flavour, of course.

Sausage Sofa

Got the wurst case of the tireds? Plop onto the most bangerin' sofa in Monstro City. (Sausage Roll pillows not included.)

Scamp - *The Froggie Doggie*

Ever wondered why a cute little puppy would want to boing around wearing a rubbery frog suit? Of course you have, but Froggie Doggies are too busy yelling 'ribbit' to answer silly questions. The best way to catch one of these jolly pooches is to tug on its pink bow because this will deflate its bizarre bouncy outfit. If that doesn't work, try popping it with a pin. Bang!

Scaramel Corn

Beyond KettleKorn Cliff lies a terrifying Dutch Oven village, where Scaramel Corn is cooked up. Dare you eat just one box?

Scare Bears

Well, they don't look too scary, but you never know with these things. Collect the whole set!

Scare-o-plane

Zoom around your new cloud room, with the scariest plane in the sky.

Scare Chair

Do you dare to sit on the scariest chair in Monstro City?

A
B
C
D
E
F
G
H
I
J
K
L
M
N
O
P
Q
R
S
T
U
V
W
X
Y
Z

Scarlet O'Haira - *The Fluffy Snuggler*

Frankly my dears, Fluffy Snugglers don't give a flying gooberry about anything apart from snuggling each other. In fact these happy little hairballs love hugging 24/7, even if the thing they're hugging can't return the favour: lamp posts, trees, random strangers, you name it. You might even wake up with a few Snugglers cosying up to your feet. Mmm!

Scare Force One

Scare Force One sure is one big airship! It is also the mobile HQ of the Criminal League Of Naughty Critters. Armed with deadly Goo Cannons, it is a terrifying sight to behold. It also comes with a handy escape pod dock, just in case things don't go according to plan for Dr. Strangeglove and his impish allies.

Scrambled Egg Backpack

You can keep all your stuff in this fetching Scrambled Egg Backpack.

Scrumpy - *The Surreal Snooper*

Say 'allo to the curious little Moshlings who just love solving mysteries and sticking their hyper-sensitive hooters into other Moshis' business. Genuinely surreal, they also enjoy riding pasta unicycles, wearing meat shoes on their heads and wrapping kippers around their waists. Bonkers!

Scummi Bears

They look wiggly jiggly, but these bears are tough as nails. New from Dastardly Delights!

A
B
C
D
E
F
G
H
I
J
K
L
M
N
O
P
Q
R
S
T
U
V
W
X
Y
Z

Sea Monster Munch

An arcade machine available at the Games Starcade. Chomp your way through as many fish as possible but be careful not to hit your own tail!

Sea Squash

Lots of stuff squashed into a delightful drink. Can be a bit salty though.

Secrets

What's the secret behind the Secrets Moshling set, that includes the likes of Roxy the Precious Prism and Blingo the Flashy Fox? Well . . . that would be telling, wouldn't it?

The Seed Cart

Located on Main Street, the Seed Cart is the place to come to buy seeds. Plant the seeds in your garden, then sit back and watch as they attract all sorts of marvellous Moshlings.

MOSHLING SEEDS

Shakesfear Bust

The most famous writer in Monstro City, author of *Groaneo and Spewliet*.

Shark Bowl

A bowl with bite!

Shark Cabinet

Watch your items don't fall in his mouth!

Shambles - *The Scrappy Chappy*

These hapless furballs look as if they've been dragged through a hedge backwards (and forwards and sideways and up and down). That's because they enjoy extreme hedge diving. When they're not somersaulting into shrubbery you'll find them nibbling their own ears. But don't worry, they grow back (and are delicious with a pucumber-based dip).

A
B
C
D
E
F
G
H
I
J
K
L
M
N
O
P
Q
R
S
T
U
V
W
X
Y
Z

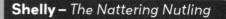

Shelly – *The Nattering Nutling*

Completely nuts? Not exactly, but Nattering Nutlings are definitely crazy ... about Moshi celebrities! Goodness knows how a Nutling would react if it bumped into Zack Binspin. When they're not singing *Music Rox* songs in front of the mirror, Nattering Nutlings love chattering to each other about the hottest new gooperstars.

Shelby – *The Slapstick Tortoise*

Slapstick Tortoises are highly-trained Moshlings. Unfortunately, whoever trained them was rubbish because the only thing they're good at is messing up their moves, falling over and ending up stuck on their shells. They can't even tie their own bandanas. And that's bad because they're supposed to be Ninjas. If only they stopped watching kung fu movies and started training, they might not be so useless. Hi-yaaa!

Shelly Splurt

Made of all things sticky and bubbly, Shelly Splurt has repeatedly earned the world-record at holding her breath. She is currently training to become a blimp at next years' Monster Carnival. She practises her craft in Monstro City's Underground Tunnels.

ShiShi – *The Sneezing Panda*

Aah-choo! These eyelash-fluttering Moshlings are obsessed with watching Monstrovision but it makes them sneeze. Lots. Experts think they are allergic to pixels. Or maybe it's the wamwoo shoots they scoff by the bucketload. When they're not glued to the screen, Sneezing Pandas are usually fiddling with magical eyedrops or scrunching up extra soft tissues.

Sherlock Nook

The original home of the Undercover YapYaps. It lies just south of Waggytail Hollow.

The Shrewman

If you go down to the woods today you might just spot the Shrewman. Shy but helpful, this berry-loving critter rarely leaves the comfort of his tree trunk home – and nor would you if you were busy writing books on your tippy-tappy typewriter. In fact some say the Shrewman uses berry juice as ink because he's too scared to go to the shops.

Shoney – *The Amazin' Blazin' Raisin*

Great balls of fire? Not quite, because these fiery fruit-based critters are actually Moshlings. Notorious for accidentally setting things on fire as they whoosh through Monstro City at breakneck speeds, Amazin' Blazin' Raisins are thought to ignite and take flight whenever they hear the phrase 'shrivelled grapes'. Twisted firestarters? You bet!

Shrillboard Magazine

The Moshi gossip mag, edited by Ruby Scribblez, that's full of celebrity tittle-tattle and photos of well-known Monsters papped by Holga the Happy Snappy.

FLASH!

Simon Growl

On the rare occurrence that Simon Growl doesn't tell you what he really thinks, you can always look at his hair to find out how he feels. Despite being voted meanest judge three years in a row, Simon is still the greatest (and only!) talent scout in Monstro City.

Skeeter Rydell

Skeeter Rydell works long hours as Gift Island's only scooter-based delivery monster. He is searching for his wife and seven children who made their home out of presents, but so far has been unable to find them.

Skidoo-Bap-Diddly-Pap Ska

Skidoo-bap-diddly-pap ska combines elements of Hoodoo Calypso and Jeepers Creepers Jazz, not to mention Roarberry Rhythm and Blues. It is characterized by a walking bassline accented with rhythms on the upbeat. Oh, and the lyrics are really just a lot of old skiddly-doo-bap nonsense.

Slop

Tastes disgusting, looks vile, that's Slop alright. It's the most popular food on sale in the Gross-ery Store … but only because it's so cheap!

Skullmunster Sneakers

Sneak your feet into some lesser-known Skullmunsters. Don't worry, they don't mind.

Slop Pipes

Install your very own Slop supply in your house! (Slop not included.)

Slime Rickey

The Slime Rickey is the slimiest drink in town – no other rickey is slimier! (It's also the chewiest!)

Slopcorn

The gunkiest movie snack around.

Sludge Fudge

Eat it fast before it drips off your plate.

Sludge Street

Having said that Main Street is the busiest bustlingest place in Monstro City, Sludge Street's not so quiet either. After all, the Monstro City Marketplace is here, so is Horrods, and Dewy's DIY shop. And then there's the Games Starcade, Sly Chance's Dodgy Dealz... There's even property to rent!

Sly Chance

Originally from The Shifty Shack Sandbar, Sly Chance was thrilled to plant his tentacles on the solid ground of Monstro City. When he's not wheelin' and dealin' over at Dodgy Dealz, he can be found at Gabby's eating quicksand-wiches.

Slug Slurp Slushie

Slug Slurp Slushies are served up by silly slitherin' slugs over at Slimy Swamp. Beware of brain freeze!

Smiley Flowers

How can you help but smile with such happy flowers?

Smilies

Happy as Larry and smiley as a sunbeam, these Moshlings can't fail to bring a smile to your face. Failing that, try saying 'the Jabbering Jibberling just jibber-jabbers jolly gibberish'. You're grinning now, aren't you?

Snap Apple

SNAP APPLE

A tricky customer this one, just as likely to take a bite out of you as you are of it, but it's the plant you're going to need to grow in your garden if you want to attract the likes of McNulty the Undercover YapYap or Honey the Funny Bunny.

Snail Ale

The slimy drink that makes you think.

Sniggerton Wood

Sniggerton Wood is where you'll find Cheeky Chimps swinging through the trees on dangling vines. You've gotta laugh, haven't you?

Snookums - *The Baby Tumteedum*

Maybe the cutest Moshlings of all, Baby Tumteedums are sweet little demi-dinos that just want to be loved. Hatched from mysterious marzipan eggs, these wide-eyed critters are always searching for someone (or something) to look after them. And that's strange because they age in reverse, so babies are actually hundreds of years old. Confused? You should be, because as well as being ancient, Baby Tumdeedums can eat two hundred yuckberries in a single day.

Snow Globe

Shake it up for your own little snow storm. Mini shovel not included.

Snowies

What's cooler than being cool? Being a sub-zero, ice-loving Snowy, that's what! The weather outside might be frightful, but the Snowies are soooo delightful, and with this Moshling set ... let it snow, let it snow, let it snow!

Snooze Cruise

Snooze Cruise is the sleepiest critter in Monstro City. Struck by a sleeping potion when he was a young sprout, he's spent 92% of his life sleeping. His snores help keep the bats away.

Snozzle Wobbleson

Snozzle Wobbleson started out as a Gross-ery Stock Monster, but everything kept slipping through his wobbly frame. He was soon promoted to cashier after dropping sixteen cartons of eggs and making a real mess of things. Snozzle loves his job and creating new and tasty treats!

Snuffy Hookums

Moshling expert extraordinaire Snuffy Hookums is Buster Bumblechops' sidekick. After disappearing under mysterious circumstances, the intrepid Moshlingologist dramatically returned to Monstro City after 1,882 days on her own in the wild, quashing rumours that she had been eaten by a tribe of dangerous Moshlings somewhere near Mount Krakkablowa.

Sooki-Yaki – *The Caped Assassin*

Now you see them, now you still see them! And that's because Caped Assassins are not as good at sneaking around as they think they are. Don't laugh because these agile little Moshlings have the ability to vanish and re-appear in an instant. The problem is they can't control their power and always pop up when they shouldn't.

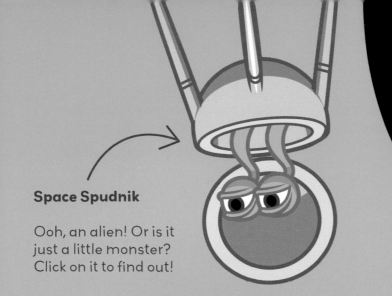

Space Spudnik

Ooh, an alien! Or is it just a little monster? Click on it to find out!

Spicy Dragon Rolls

Not for the faint of heart, wasabi-powered Spicy Dragon Rolls really turn up the heat!

Spider Chandelier

A spider that hangs from your ceiling, appropriately enough.

Spider Dartboard

Webbed fun for all the family. (Not suitable for flies under twelve.)

Spineapple

If you've never tried Spineapple on pizza, then you must! Or just throw some on your wall.

Spider Lolly

Eight crunchy legs of bristle-haired flavour. YUM!

Splatter – *The Abstract Artiste*

Is it art or an utter shambles? Who cares because every Abstract Artiste's ambition is to win the coveted Blurgh-ner Prize For Bafflingly Bonkers Art. That's why these crazy Moshlings spend all day flicking gluey glitter at passers-by and pickling slices of Oobla Doobla in huge tanks of fluorescent jelly. Magnifique!

Splutnik

With his trusty jetpack, Splutnik is the hyperactive Zoshling capable of rocketing from one side of the Silky Way to the other in less than twelve argh-secs. Besides serving as chief engineer aboard the *Rhapsody 2*, this bubble-brained geek is a kazoo maestro, and is the Zoshling who discovered the 'Bossanova Goopernova' (whatever that is) when he was still a space cadet.

Spookies

This supernatural set of Moshlings includes Woolly Blue Hoodoos, Furry Heebees, Fancy Banshees and the cutest Baby Ghost you ever saw ... Or did you? Perhaps you're seeing things! Do-do-do-do, do-do-do-do ...

Spookies Haunted Hostel

Made of thirty per cent Wobble-Plasma, the Haunted Hostel is the perfect Spookies habitat.

Squidge - *The Furry Heebee*

Super cute? Not really. A Furry Heebee's bite is worse than its bark. That's because these flying Moshlings are greedy bloodsuckers that flutter around at night hunting for juicy victims. When they can't find any necks to nip, they'll settle for a nice mug of instant tomato soup with plenty of garlicky croutons. Oh yes, about the bark: it's more of a high-pitched 'mwah-ha-ha' but it's still enough to give you goosebumps!

Sprockett and Hubbs

A
B
C
D
E
F
G
H
I
J
K
L
M
N
O
P
Q
R
S
T
U
V
W
X
Y
Z

Accident-prone creators of some of C.L.O.N.C.'s most dastardly contraptions (including various Glumping machines), Sprockett and Hubbs are the untrustworthy robotic duo who can't stop squabbling. In fact they can't even agree on who to work for. Put it this way, if you oil their cogs they'll do your jobs!
Hubbs is the hyperactive little bubblehead inventor who can't stop babbling on about oil cocktails and circuit board sandwiches whilst flitting around on his rollerball. Maybe he has a screw loose? Sprockett is the serious lunk with a short fuse who seems to think he's the brains behind S&H Industries. Sadly his central processor is about the size of a shrivelled splatsuma (but don't tell him that).

Squiff

What's got three eyes, buck teeth and stupid hair? Squiff, of course! This naughty nugget might be golden but when it comes to being friendly Squiff is worthless, especially when letting rip with a Squiffy Stinkbomb! Urgh!

Stacey Grace

Stacey Grace attends Miss Jingle's School for Girls and waits for her classmates on the bridge at The Port. She has a small problem with tying her shoelaces, and sometimes trips and falls. Thankfully, her mother lets her go to school in bare feet.

Stanley - *The Songful SeaHorse*

Although they are very cute, Songful SeaHorses are also incredibly annoying. That's because they can't stop whistling awful show tunes at ear-splitting volume. Each tune is usually accompanied by a barrage of bubbles and a silly dance. Experts believe they're trying to attract other SeaHorses but no one can stand the racket long enough to find out.

Star Blossom

This radiant bloom is what you'll need if you're hoping to trap Squidge the Furry Heebee or catch Snookums the Baby Tumteedum.

Star Clock

Like stars? Like gold? Like to know the time? Guess what, this is for you!

Star Dressing Room Door

The perfect room door for any budding Monstar!

Star Glasses

You're a star, so let everyone know with these funky star glasses.

Star Light Lamp

Not counting the Sun, the best star to read a book with.

Starfishbucks Coffee

Starfishbucks is where Moshlings can go to grab a drink. Cali the Valley Mermaid hangs out there a lot. If you want to put up a poster on the noticeboard inside, just don't ask them if they've got any tacks!

Starlight Cookies

The biscuits that fell to Earth. Perfect for eating in the dark.

Stashley Snoozer

Stashley often appears to be sleeping, but stays attentive 24/7 through the clever use of his hat, which can see everything, everywhere, every moment. So don't try anything funny!

STARFISHBUCKS COFFEE

STARFISHBUCKS COFFEE

"SUN SMASHER 9000"

Rock Hard PVC

Liquid Rox powered core

Turbo rocket booster

Doom Fist

Navigation system

Rugged rudder

The Stinker

Pee-ew! Well, it's famous but man, does that statue stink!

Strudel Station

The Strudel Station is the natural habitat of Scrumpy and other Surreal Snoopers.

Sun Smasher 9000

One of Dr. Strangeglove's monstrous machines, the Sun Smasher 9000 is made up of a turbo rocket booster powered by a liquid Rox core, a giant boxing glove made of rock hard PVC … and that's pretty much it. It's designed to do exactly what it says on the tin … and that's to smash the sun! Knockout!

Suey - *The Bashful Bowlhead*

Feeling peckish? Then why not hook up with a Bashful Bowlhead because these shy Moshlings produce a never-ending supply of slurp-tastic noodles from their bowl-like bonces. You'll need a knife and fork because their chopsticks are actually sensitive feelers used to sense danger.

Super Diavlo

Hands on your hips, puff out your chest and … run for cover, because if Super Diavlo's on the case you're sure to feel the full force of a Phenomenal Firestarter, especially if this volcanic hothead is angry. Smokin'!

A
B
C
D
E
F
G
H
I
J
K
L
M
N
O
P
Q
R
S
T
U
V
W
X
Y
Z

Super Furi

If Super Furi's on the case you can be sure the fur will fly because this hairy hero is tougher than a bag of hammers! With plenty of fuzz to cushion the bashes, Super Furi is probably the strongest superhero in town!

Super Glooper Day

Super Glooper Day is an annual Moshi festival based on the legendary Gloop Monster – a mythical character from Moshi folklore! Citizens of Monstro City hold gloop parties where they scoff Gloop Soup, and leave buckets outside in the hope the Gloop Monster will leave a yucky surprise.

Super Katsuma

Faster than a Wheelie YumYum and more powerful than a billion Baby Blockheads, Super Katsuma is the slick hero who can bash baddies in seconds with a Kung Fu Frenzy. Look out for those claws or you'll be sliced and diced in no time!

Super Luvli

Look, up in the sky! Is it a Birdie? Is it a SkyPony? No it's Super Luvli, the flutterly amazing Super Moshi whose star-tipped stem strikes fear into baddies. Prepare to be bamboozled by a Shimmering Sparkle Shower!

'Super Moshi March'

As well as saving Moshi world from the machinations of Dr. Strangeglove and the other villainous members of C.L.O.N.C., the Super Moshis have also recorded a stirring march, which appears on the *Music Rox* album. It has since become their official theme tune!

Super Moshiversity

This is the university in the Moshi world that everyone who wants to become a Super Moshi attends. Famous alumni include Elder Furi and Dr. Strangeglove (although he's rather more infamous than famous).

Super Poppet

Too bashful to battle baddies? No way, because Super Poppet's boots were made for stomping as well as dancing! Better still, this cuddly crime fighter can boogie on out of almost any situation, especially when performing an Up and Away Whirl.

The Super Moshis

Is it a bird? Is it a plane? Is it some guy wearing his pants outside his trousers? No! It's the Super Moshis! These highly-trained Moshi Monsters work as a team to thwart the plans of C.L.O.N.C. – particularly Dr. Strangeglove and his minions, the Glumps. Guided by Elder Furi they fight for right and to uphold the Heroes' Code.

A B C D E F G H I J K L M N O P Q R S T U V W X Y Z

Super Seeds

If you head on over to The Port you can get yourself some Super Seeds. Crazy Daises or Snap Apples, either will do, and then, when you plant them, you could find yourself cultivating a Rare Moshling!

Super Zommer

Are you ready to rock? Good, because Super Zommer is ready to roll, any time, any place. Despite an appetite for goo and a thirst for wobble-ade this laid back rocker is a master of the Stitch Pick Super Kick. Yeah!

Sweet Tooth

Quick, grab your toothbrush because Sweet Tooth is the sugary psycho who's mad, bad and dangerous to slurp. As a leading member of C.L.O.N.C. this deliciously evil candy criminal never goes anywhere without a big bag of tooth-rotting treats and a Hypno Blaster lollipop. But is Sweet Tooth a he or a she? Who knows because the last monster to ask is still in moshpital, wearing a gobstopper! Sweet Tooth likes licking lollipops and combing cotton candy, but has an aversion to savoury snacks – and dentists!

'Sweet Tooth Stomp'

The sugar-obsessed villain's gooey glam rock contribution to the *Music Rox* album. It's so catchy that once you've heard it, it gets stuck in your head like bubblegum gets stuck in your fur!

A
B
C
D
E
F
G
H
I
J
K
L
M
N
O
P
Q
R
S
T
U
V
W
X
Y
Z

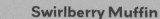

Swirlberry Muffin

Winner of the Tallest Swirl of the year award.

Switchy Day

This is the one day in the year when everything is switchified. Monsters dress up like their owners, owners dress up like their monsters, and everyone walks, talks, eats and sleeps . . . the wrong way round! Yako?

Swooniverse

The Moshi world is not alone. There are other planets out there, like Symphonia and Space Glenn, but they are all contained within the infinitely vast Swooniverse.

Symphonia

Home planet of the musical alien Zoshlings.

Tt

TakiTaki Islands

Home of the Disco Duckie Moshlings.

Talk Like A Pirate Day

Speak like Cap'n Buck E. Barnacle for just one day out of the entire year. Aarrrr!

Tamara Tesla

Reared in a giant petri dish in Variable Valley, Tamara Tesla is Monstro City's own brainy scientist. She has a lab set up at the Observatory at The Port, where she invents new puzzles for the Puzzle Palace.

Tash

If you consider your monster to be a totally spiffing chap (or you secretly fancy giving them a Strangeglove makeover) then you need this piece of kit – a totally terrific and twirl-able tash!

Teardrop Earring

Far west of Monstro City, these teardrop earrings fall from the weepiest tree of all.

FL*A*SH!

Techies

Where would we be without modern technology? More importantly, where would the Moshi world be without this set of teeny tiny Techies? Need to call your Monster friends? The Mini Moshifone is for you. Want to take a picture? You need a Happy Snappy. Need a hand? Better call a Titchy TrundleBot!

Tentacle Chair

You'll find it hard to stand up when the suckers get you!

Tentacle Torch

Light your way with this ever so slightly creepy tentacle torch.

Techies Glitchy Gazebo

Add a jolt of awesome to your room with the Techies Glitchy Gazebo. Buzzz, blip, zoink!

A B C D E F G H I J K L M N O P Q R S T U V W X Y Z

Thump a Glump

The aim of the game is simple – you just have to splat every Glump you see!

Tiara

If your monster dresses like a princess, acts like a princess, and thinks she is a princess then give her a tiara and everyone else will know she's a perfect poppet of a princess, too.

Tiamo - *The Sparkly Sweetheart*

Shhh ... hear that? It's the gentle pulse of a Sparkly Sweetheart. These magical Moshlings often appear from nowhere to help monsters in distress with their sparkling energy auras. When they are not performing life-saving magic they love d-dumfing to power ballads.

Tiddles

Tiddles is a local legend. He started as bait on Billy Bob Baitman's hook, but escaped the clutches of an old boot and fed on algae at the bottom of the lake, growing to 1,500 times his normal size! Tiddles now entertains the locals with his beautifully yodelled songs.

Tiki - *The Pilfering Toucan*

Colourful but crafty, Pilfering Toucans can't resist 'borrowing' things from fellow Moshlings, especially salty gobstoppers. When we say borrow, we actually mean steal because these thieving flappers are the naughtiest pirates on the planet. You won't believe how quickly they can swipe your pocket money and stash it in their beaks. Maybe it's because Pilfering Toucans once sailed the seventy seas alongside some of the meanest Moshi Monsters in history. Aarrr!

Tiki Torch

Strike a light! If you're going to go exploring ruined temples in the Gombala Gombala Jungle, taking one of these with you would be a bright idea. After all, you never know when a Tiki Torch might just match your needs perfectly.

Tingaling - *The Kitten of Good Fortune*

Good fortune befalls any monster who stumbles upon a Kitten of Good Fortune, particularly if its magic neck bell is tinkling. Remember to wave if you see one because these mystic Moshlings can spread joy and happiness with just one wave of the paw.

Toad In The Hole

Freshest toad (hole not included).

Toasty - *The Buttery Breadhead*

The greatest thing since sliced bread? Not exactly because these happy-go-lucky Moshlings enjoy spreading salty butter across their faces before leaping off tall buildings and trying to land butter side up. Crumbs! Buttery Breadheads hate the cold so don't be surprised if you catch one hiding in your toaster.

Toad Soda

From the makers of Croak-a-cola. Contains real toad.

Tomba - *The Wistful Snowtot*

Feeling chilly? There must be a Wistful Snowtot nearby. Made of ice, snow and stuff we don't know, these frosty Moshlings are usually glum – hardly surprising as abominable critters are always kicking them to bits. Heartbrrr-eaking!

A
B
C
D
E
F
G
H
I
J
K
L
M
N
O
P
Q
R
S
T
U
V
W
X
Y
Z

Toffee Crunch Couch

Slip and slide as you sit!

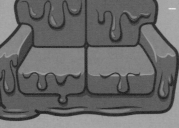

TomaSquawk

TomaSquawk is the vicious cuckoo that lives in Big Chief Tiny Head's feathery headdress. He's heap big trouble!

Topsy Turvy - *The Tardy Timer*

Time waits for no Moshi, especially Tardy Timers because they are always running late. And that's weird because the powdered egg running through their hourglass figures is rumoured to tickle their tummies whenever they are delayed. Then again, you'd probably be late too if you spent all day doing handstands yelling 'Ooh, it tickles!'

Totem Troll

A Mystic
Monster
Totem Troll.

Trashcan Surprise

Every bite is a taste bud
adventure! Just make
sure you hold your nose . . .

Traditional Turkoy

Oh yes, for
Thanksgiving there
must be Turkoy. Like
a leg? There are six
to choose from.

Treasure Chest

Aarrr, did I hear ye speak of Ye
Treasurey Cheste? Full of gold it is,
me hearties!

Train Set

Click on it and watch the train go
round and round. Hey, the journey
is the destination!
Choo choo!

A
B
C
D
E
F
G
H
I
J
K
L
M
N
O
P
Q
R
S
T
U
V
W
X
Y
Z

Tribal Masks

Ancient monsters wore these masks to hide their faces, but no one could tell the difference.

Tunies

Strike up the band – it's the most harmonious of Moshlings, the Tunies! They like nothing better than making sweet music together, and if you have one in your Moshling Zoo you can join them, and rock out with the band!

Trixie

Native to the slime streams of the Underground Tunnels, Trixie enjoys nibbling at algae growths and fickle ferns. This rare breed of fish can change its colours to match any in the rainbow, and therefore spends its time wherever rainbows gather.

Twistmas

Get in the festive spirit every year as your monster celebrates Twistmas – the Moshi Christmas!

A
B
C
D
E
F
G
H
I
J
K
L
M
N
O
P
Q
R
S
T
U
V
W
X
Y
Z

Twistmas Kandy Kanes

Twist and turn
as you chew this
Twistmassy Kandy.

Twistmas Pudding

With this Twistmas Pudding you'll
end up stretching your stomach and
twisting your tongue!

Tyra Fangs

Runway model, TV
show host, and gossip
queen, Tyra Fangs hails
from Goo York, but now
spends her days in
Monstro City with her
boyfriend Roary Scrawl,
editor of *The Daily
Growl*. She loves facials,
shopping, and bossing
Roary around.

Tyre Swing

Just like the one
your momma
monster put
up in the
garden. Oh the
good old days!

A
B
C
D
E
F
G
H
I
J
K
L
M
N
O
P
Q
R
S
T
U
V
W
X
Y
Z

The Underground Disco

Uncle Scallops
- *The Cranky Codfather*

Rumoured to have once ruled the legendary city of Splatlantis, Cranky Codfathers are now better known for prodding passers-by with their plastic tridents. Well you'd be cranky too if you spent all day helping Moshlings across the road. Yep, that's right, these fishy fellas work as crossing guards on busy Haddock Highway.

The Underground Disco

The most exclusive nightspot in Monstro City, the Underground Disco is located within the sewers, its entrance guarded by Bubba the Bouncer. If your name's not down, you're not coming in. If you are admitted to the coolest club in town your Moshi Monster can get funky to the latest bad beats and smooth tunes.

Unknown Zone

For somewhere called the Unknown Zone, everyone seems to know where it is! It's where the Zoshling spaceship *Rhapsody 2* crash-landed.

Vv

Vampy's Fangs

A Vampy isn't a Vampy without zis pair of vicious-looking fangs.

Vanity Table

For when you just want to stare at yourself in the mirror. Oh, aren't I beautiful?!

Volcano

This active volcano contains the Super Moshi super-secret super HQ. Monsters hoping to become Super Moshis have to make it past the Gatekeeper before being permitted to train under the guidance of Elder Furi.

A
B
C
D
E
F
G
H
I
J
K
L
M
N
O
P
Q
R
S
T
U
V
W
X
Y
Z

Ww

Wall Bats

One of Monstro City's most spooktacular items. Just make sure they don't give your Monster a fright!

Waldo - *The Tabby Nerdicat*

A Tabby Nerdicat can tell you the square root of a banana in a flash but thinks being cool means sitting in a bucket of ice. They spend most days (and nights) fiddling with circuit boards, arguing over geeky comics and listening to 'Quantum Physics Hour' on Fangdoodle FM. Trying to find a Tabby Nerdicat is harder than reverse algebra but they seem to like toffee nachos. Never ask 'em to dance. They can't.

Wallop - *The Jolly Tubthumper*

Bashing yourself in the face with a pair of drumsticks isn't crazy – it's totally bonkers! But where else are these tip-tapping Moshlings supposed to practise their paradiddles? Besides, Jolly Tubthumpers love drumming, and their thwacktastic bodies are brilliantly boingy. Drum roll please!

A
B
C
D
E
F
G
H
I
J
K
L
M
N
O
P
Q
R
S
T
U
V
W
X
Y
Z

ABCDEFGHIJKLM
NOPQRSTUVWXYZ

WallScrawl

WallScrawl are letters
and pictures you can put
on your wall as decoration.
They can be purchased from
Babs' Boutique.

Wavey Davey

Waving to everyone and everything
in Monstro City is Wavey Davey's
favourite pastime. After
wearing out his best arm, he
ate plenty of Green, built it
back up and has resumed
to a happy status of
waving it proudly. He
enjoys high-fives, down-
lows, too-slows, and all
variations of hellos.

Weevil Kneevil

Weevil Kneevil is Main Street's only courier. He delivers parcels between Yukea and Bizarre Bazaar. Some whisper that he's delivering love letters between the shopkeepers, but Weevil swears it's only his prize-winning pickled blueberry rings.

'Welcome to Jollywood'

Bobbi SingSong's breakthrough single that appears on the *Music Rox* album. Be warned, this infectious track just might send you quite doolally!

Westmonster Abbey

Teeny TickTocks can often be spotted on the foggy banks near Westmonster Abbey.

Where's I.G.G.Y.?

Join Katsuma and Poppet in this mini game as they search for missing I.G.G.Y. across the Moshi wilderness. Finding him won't be easy, and you'll suspect there's more to I.G.G.Y.'s disappearance than meets the eye . . .

A
B
C
D
E
F
G
H
I
J
K
L
M
N
O
P
Q
R
S
T
U
V
W
X
Y
Z

White Fang - *The Musky Husky*

Totally barking and slightly whiffy, Musky Huskies are the tail-chasing, bone-loving tearaways that will do almost anything for a bite to eat. They've even been spotted rummaging through trash cans searching for scraps. Maybe that's why they always look so scruffy – why groom when you can scoff? Take care if you decide to pet one of these greedy mucky pups – it might bite off your delicious looking fingers. Grrrrrr!

Whoopie Cushion

Sneakily slip this under a cushion and wait for someone to sit down ... Paaarp!

Wiggy Thingy

The Wiggy Thingy is the furry creature that sits on top of Simon Growl's head, keeping his bald bonce warm at the same time as saving the music mogul's blushes. It has also been known to cast a vote at the talent contests that take place in the Underground Disco, and has been seen getting its groove on when Simon takes a turn at spinning the discs.

A
B
C
D
E
F
G
H
I
J
K
L
M
N
O
P
Q
R
S
T
U
V
W
X
Y
Z

Wiggy Wonderland

One of the hairiest places Cap'n Buck has ever visited.

Wing, Fang, Screech and Sonar

Exiled from Ecto's Cave after terrifying Monstro City residents, siblings Wing, Fang, Screech and Sonar are the Underground Tunnel's premier bat residents. They keep watch for gossip to report to *The Daily Growl*.

Wiz Hat

A monstrously magical Wizard's hat. Alakazam!

Woolly - *The Titchy-Tusked Mammoth*

Titchy-Tusked Mammoths spend most evenings dyeing their pelts with inka inka essence and dipping their ears and feet in gloopy green puddles. These snuffly Moshlings can even remove their woolly blue coats if it gets too warm and unscrew their tusks (which they sharpen using snooker cue chalk).

A B C D E F G H I J K L M N O P Q R S T U V W X Y Z

Worldies

I've been around the world but I-I-I've never seen Moshlings like these before. There are four of these little monumental wonders to collect.

Worldies Planetary Palace

Around the world in eighty days? Well, maybe having the Planetary Palace is good enough.

Wurley - *The Twirly Tiddlycopter*

Thanks to their motory-rotory headgear, these tin-skinned flying Moshlings are always in demand, especially when they are transporting Rox and other precious thingies across the world of Moshi. As they wokka-wokka through the clouds, Tiddlycopters love humming classical music and performing loop-the-loops. Don't mention Dr. Strangeglove – he tricked an entire squadron of Tiddlies into powering his diabolical glumping machine with their spinning tailfins. Nooo!

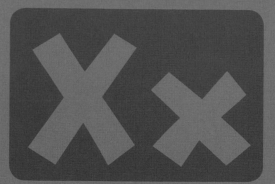

X

One of the WallScrawl Alphabet, but what will you spell with an X? Maybe 'xylophone'.

Yellow Bowler Ball

The best dressed ball on the lane, in sunburnt yellow. (Also available in striped yellow!)

Yolka - *The Boiled Boffin*

When is an egg not an egg? When it's a Boiled Boffin of course! Brainy beyond belief, these eggheady Moshlings are renowned for their goopendous ability to remember anything, from the number of shoes worn by seventy splatterpillars to the exact time of Furbert Snufflepeeps' disappearance – but only if they are wearing their magic spectacles!

Yy

Younger Furi

Younger Furi was the best friend of one Lavender Troggs while the two of them were studying at Super Moshiversity. He eventually grew up to become Elder Furi.

Yukea

Yukea on Main Street is Monstro City's favourite furniture shop, run by Moe Yukky. It's got everything you need to get your monster's home set up, from floors and wallpapers to seating and shelves.

Yoyo - *The Creative Coyote*

Not to be confused with Hoxy Foxies, Creative Coyotes love making things, from yoghurt pot rockets to sausage skin legwarmers. When they're not busy starting new trends these hip little Moshlings enjoy painting silly slogans on walls by dipping their bushy tails in paint. Swish!

A
B
C
D
E
F
G
H
I
J
K
L
M
N
O
P
Q
R
S
T
U
V
W
X
Y
Z

Zz

Ziggy - *The Quirky Koala*

Pump up the glam because Quirky Koalas are the music-loving Moshlings that enjoy face-painting and stomping around to flamboyant old songs. If you see one sprinkling glitter on the ground, don't worry – it's probably preparing to mark its territory by performing a signature glitter angel.

Zack Binspin
- *The Moptop Tweenybop*

Zack Binspin has dreamt of being a famous singer ever since he saw Screech McPiehole yelling on *Top of the Mops*. And now, thanks to his high-trousered mentor Simon Growl, that dream is finally a reality. Zack used to sing backing vocals for one of Monstro City's biggest bin-bound singers, but solo gooperstardom beckoned the second he was signed by HighPants Productions.

Zoinks

This mischief-maker has decided to give shopkeeping a go! When he's not stacking shelves with spooky stuff, this dearly departed troublemaker plays poltergeist pranks on customers! Glow in the dark larks? You betcha!

ZOMMER

Zommer's Drop
Dead Threads

Zommers

Don't freak out when you see a
Zommer! They're the stitch-picking,
drool-licking thingamajigs who are all
of a jumble. They can't remember why
they are falling apart at the
seams, but they still know
how to rock out!

Zommers love dressing up, especially
to celebrate Halloween, and where
else would they buy their outfits from
other than Zommer's Drop Dead
Threads? They wouldn't be seen dead
wearing anything else! This shop stocks
some more unusual items, including
eyepieces and worm earrings!

Zoot Fruit

You ain't never seen a
jazzier banana. Just
don't tell him he's a fruit.

Zoshlings

Cute and cuddly aliens
from the musical planet
of Symphonia.

A
B
C
D
E
F
G
H
I
J
K
L
M
N
O
P
Q
R
S
T
U
V
W
X
Y
Z

191

Aa-Zz